Leigh Hunt and
What is Poetry?

Leigh Hunt and
What is Poetry?

ROMANTICISM AND THE PURPOSE OF POETRY

FLEMMING OLSEN

sussex
ACADEMIC
PRESS
Brighton • Portland • Toronto

2 4 6 8 10 9 7 5 3 1

First published 2011 in Great Britain in the United Kingdom by
SUSSEX ACADEMIC PRESS
PO Box 139   Eastbourne BN24 9BP

and in the United States of America by
SUSSEX ACADEMIC PRESS
920 NE 58th Ave Suite 300
Portland, Oregon 97213–3786

and in Canada by
SUSSEX ACADEMIC PRESS (CANADA)
90 Arnold Avenue, Thornhill, Ontario L4J 1B5

British Library Cataloguing in Publication Data
A CIP catalogue record for this book is available from the British Library.

Library of Congress Cataloguing-in-Publication Data
Olsen, Flemming.
Leigh Hunt and What is poetry? : romanticism and the purpose of poetry /
    Flemming Olsen.
p. cm.
Includes bibliographical references and index.
ISBN 978-1-84519-443-7 (p/b : alk. paper)
    1. Hunt, Leigh, 1784–1859—Criticism and interpretation. 2. English
poetry—19th century—History and criticism. 3. Romanticism—Great
Britain. I. Title.
PR4814.O47 2011
821'.7—dc22   2010032592

Papers used by Sussex Academic Press are natural, renewable and recyclable
products from well-managed forests and certified in accordance with
the rules of the Forest Stewardship Council.

Typeset by Sussex Academic Press, Brighton & Eastbourne.
Printed TJ International, Padstow, Cornwall.
This book is printed on acid-free paper.

Contents

Preface

Thirty years after Leigh Hunt's death, Arthur Symons wrote, in his edition of Hunt's essays (1890): "The position of Leigh Hunt in our literature might easily be exaggerated, and still more easily underestimated".[1] That cryptic appraisal says nothing about Hunt's actual position. Yet it contains a core of truth in that Hunt's reputation as a poet and a critic has oscillated between the two extremes of exaggeration and underestimation.

When he was young and promising, he was on very friendly terms with Byron, Keats, and especially Shelley, all of whom admired his poetry as well as his ardent desire for political reform. He acted as literary midwife to Keats and Shelley, who first had their first poems published in one of Hunt's periodicals. Byron praised his *Rimini* poem, and it was in Hunt's home that Shelley and Keats first met in 1816.

However, by the second decade of the 19th century, when Hunt was in his early thirties, a perceptible change set in. Byron modified his laudatory evaluation of *The Story of Rimini* considerably; Keats criticized some of Hunt's poems for their peculiar vocabulary, Shelley gradually limited himself to praising the moral quality of Hunt's verse; Wordsworth, who had never been a great admirer of Hunt's poetical achievement, distanced himself unequivocally from Hunt, and in 1817 *Blackwood's* magazine struck home by appointing Hunt leader of the Cockney School of Poetry.

Admittedly, the rapid decline was not unconnected with the scepticism bordering on actual dislike felt towards Hunt the man by his contemporaries. However, from a literary point of view, the whipping-boy designation is largely understandable and not undeserved: Hunt's poetry is characterized by verbosity and, frequently, by a quasi-preposterous vocabulary of his own making – the butt of *Blackwood's* lambasting. His dramas are at best insipid and consequently short-lived. Many of his contributions to periodicals, of which he edited a considerable number, breathe the spirit of a hedonistic and superficial feel good atmosphere.

It is true that in his reviews of plays, ballets and operas he sometimes gives vivid – and, to posterity, valuable – assessments of the performances of individual actors, dancers and singers, and it would be misleading to call him an ignoramus in matters theatrical, but he had next to nothing to offer in the way of understanding and interpreting the nature and essence of drama.

From about 1818 and nearly two hundred years onwards, the name of Leigh Hunt evoked in literary critics the image of a second-rate poet who is chiefly remembered for exercising a harmful influence on Keats and for sponging off his friends. He was compared with, and seen in terms of, Byron, Keats and Shelley – hence came to be looked upon as an extra on the illustrious Romantic stage, where actors beyond his compass were performing with such virtuosity. Critics who refer to him at all treat him as the surface-riding epigone of the great Romantic poets, whose contemporary he had had the good fortune to be, and whom, by a stroke of good luck, he survived, which conferred on him, in his later life, the status and prestige of a grey eminence: he might not be a poetical genius, but he had rubbed shoulders with the Really Great Ones.

Until the beginning of the 21st century, academia did not take a great interest in Hunt's work. It is true that George Saintsbury granted Hunt "almost the first place in a history of prosody",[2] but generally speaking he was not in the focus of literary research.

However, the first decade of the 21st century has seen some attempts to rehabilitate this uncanonical writer. The *London Review of Books* from 2003 talks about "the growing awareness of the significant contribution (Hunt) made to poetry and belles letters", and he is referred to as "one of the most important radical journalists of the early 19th century.[3] In their biographies (both from 2005), Nicholas Roe and Anthony Holden try to restore Hunt to what they consider his rightful prominence as a journalist. They endeavour to change the uniformly negative picture of Hunt that has prevailed for so long. However, their efforts are almost exclusively devoted to Hunt's journalistic career, and here, it seems to me, the pendulum has swung from "undervaluing" to "exaggeration". Roe and Holden have very little to say about Hunt's poetical achievement, and they do not try to assess his poetry or his literary criticism. Thus, neither of them make even the briefest reference to *What Is Poetry?*

The present book is an analysis of Hunt's greatest achievement within literary criticism, viz. the long essay *What Is Poetry?*, which, for all its weaknesses, deserves a place among Romantic theories of poetry. The essay has not been dealt with at any length before, and my interest in it was prompted by the natural question whether the unanimously reserved or downright condescending criticism of Hunt and his oeuvre might not have overshadowed or ignored something valuable in his output. Could there be some respects in which he had been, in Symons' phrasing "undervalued" as a literary critic?

Leigh Hunt and
What is Poetry?

I

The Man

Bits of autobiographical information are scattered throughout Hunt's works. However, the best way to get closer to the man would seem to be to look into his autobiography, which was published in 1850.

"The present work originated in necessity, was commenced with unwillingness, has taken several years of illness and interruption to write, repeatedly moved me to ask the publisher to let me change it for another," he writes[1] in the preface without specifying what caused his reluctance to undertake the task, or what he would have preferred to do instead. The autobiography shows Hunt as a comparatively modest man who was throughout his life plagued by intermittent fits of ill health. "I claim no importance for anything I have done or undergone," he says on the first page.[2] Still, his modesty was balanced by a certain amount of assertiveness. Born in 1784, he began as a drama critic as early as in 1805, but frankly admits that at that time he did not know even the first thing about drama.[3] And yet, he adds, "most of my assessments have proved valid to this day" (i.e. 1850). That is not a vain boast, for a modern reader is inclined to agree with him.

His autobiography shows Hunt as a man of huge reading and enthusiasm who generously shared his extensive fingertip knowledge with generations of fellow poets, budding writers and readers. Browning's epitaph of him says "Write me as one who loves his fellow men."

However, a good deal of naïveté went into his kind-heartedness: he did not understand Keats' irritation with him, and he was amazed when Byron took umbrage at his revelations in *Lord Byron and Some of his Contemporaries*; he protested that he had written nothing that he had not told Byron to his face, and he was genuinely astonished at his friends' growing impatience with his financial carelessness. Therefore his statement in his autobiography – which came out when he was well into his sixties – "I have no enemies"[4] stretches credulity too far: it is patently wrong.

He could be a biting polemicist, for example in his vituperations against the Prince Regent's debauchery, which aroused the enmity of the Royal Family as well as many influential people; or in his retort to the *Quarterly* and *Blackwood's*, which for years picked on him for being the leader of the Cockney School of Poetry. It is only fair to add, though, that those periodicals did not pull their punches. Thus, in 1817, *Blackwood's* characterized *The Story of Rimini* (1816) as "the genteel comedy of incest", and insinuated that the story was based on Hunt's own experiences.

Hunt was a sincerely religious man, who calls the universe "the palpable revelation . . . of God",[5] and who was convinced that the world was witnessing a new religious revival, viz. "the religion of loving Duty to God and Man".[6] He voices an Enlightenment-like optimism: "All that has happened in the world may have been the best for all of us in the long run."[7]

Hunt's autobiography contains next to nothing about poetry – his own or that of other poets – or literary theory and criticism. Even more remarkably, he is very reticent about his private life. He corrected the spelling mistakes of his future wife's love letters and sent them back to her for correction. He leaves no doubt about his sincere love for her though she was not the intellectual type, but it is also obvious that he expected a generous measure of admiration from her. Curiously enough, his really warm words about her only appear in his obituary of her.[8] The births of his many children are unsentimentally recorded, and the death of one of his sons is given a brief, but warm, three-line comment. That forms a stark contrast to the detailed descriptions of the travelling experiences of the family and of the many places where they lived.

Altogether, the autobiography shows us Hunt as a happy, albeit somewhat naïve and absent-minded family man even though he was far from always the one who brought home the bacon.

Hunt's oeuvre, together with information from contemporary sources, permits us to piece together more of a life-size portrait than is furnished by the autobiography.

"He saw everything through books, or he saw it dimly," his son Thornton said about him. He wrote his first poems when he was ten, and at the age of 16 he won a prize for a translation of Horace. Around that time, too, he began to study Italian. During the whole of his lifetime he drank avidly, but not deeply, of the Pierian spring. He never became a really learned man, but his extensive reading enabled him to quote famous as well as less known English and foreign, including classical, authors. He translated Greek, Latin and Italian writers, and even if he was as much of a *traditore* is his work as a *traduttore* – he tended to render the originals in his own idiosyncratic idiom, irrespective of their age and background – his translations were inspired by a genuine wish to improve the general reader's taste by bringing him into contact with some of the masterpieces of the human spirit. He was a very industrious man, engaged in different kinds of writing for upwards of 60 years, and he died from overwork in 1859.

In many respects he was a tolerant man: he took up the cudgels for Shelley, and he passed Byron's stab in the back over the stay in Italy over in silence. He gave a nuancéd portrait of Sheridan, eulogizing him for his speeches and his talent as a dramatic critic, but tactfully deploring his drinking habits.

As a theatre critic he strove to be impartial, and he never associated with the actors and actresses whose performances he reviewed. His theatrical and operatic reviews – and they are reviews, not criticism – are in character. He addressed the task with an ardent, almost contagious, pleasure, and the reader feels in company with a person who knows *something*, and who wants to convey his impressions as precisely as possible. Hunt not only has an eye for what any intelligent, self-taught person would see, but, on top of that, his articles are spiced with what he considered significant details of observation: this dancer's performance of a pirouette (occasionally he dabbled in ballet reviews), that singer's mistaken rendering of a vowel sound, and that actor's marvellous body language when reciting a line from Shakespeare. It is true that he was one of the first to see Edmund Kean's talent, but in his treatment of plays and operas as a whole we seldom reach below the surface. Admittedly, his reviews testify to his extensive reading, but he reverts again and again to some favourite themes of his, for example the generally deplorable state of the noble art of acting (his opinion of what the desirable standard would be only appears indirectly), and the need of building better theatres and providing more light in them. But then again, he was never really malicious.

The torrent of essays that he contributed to the numerous periodicals for which he was partly or wholly responsible are not like, for example, Montaigne's or Bacon's reflections on the great issues of life. Where Montaigne said, "Je suis moy-mesme le sujet de mon livre", Hunt never makes his own person the subject of an essay. Of course his opinions shine through, but they are mostly about trivia, like the latest fashion in ladies' wear, or a remark he overheard in the street. But he never puts such observations into any kind of perspective. His essays are indebted to Addison's and Steele's *Spectator* essays, but Hunt never discusses questions of morality (like Steele's picture of "an old Beau in Town") or criticism (like Addison's "The Pleasures of the Imagination").

In the *Examiner* Hunt gives an ironic status report of the tone prevalent in some periodicals of the day. "If you cannot reach your adversary's head, aim directly at his heart, and in the intervals of the battle amuse yourself by calling him names." That was not Hunt's approach.

Hunt was always more concerned with the result than with the process. He was a popularizer, and he made no secret of the fact that his target group was the general reader, whose characteristics or preferences are, however, never specified. He appears as a benevolent, albeit somewhat otherworldly, optimist: in the Preface to the *Examiner* (1808) we read that the intention of the periodical is to "encourage an unprejudiced spirit of thinking in every respect", and that the ultimate object is "truth" (again a rather vague term). However, the *Examiner* acquired a certain reputation as a poetical magazine, and some of Hunt's most perspicacious political writing was printed there.

In his youth he won a reputation as a political reformer, but his politics was sentiment at least as much as reflection. He had no coherent political vision but was frequently urged by a strong social indignation. He wanted to assist in bringing about a reform in Parliament, he says in his autobiography,[9] but in the same sentence he derails the idea and confuses the issue: "and a fusion of literary taste into all subjects whatever."

What sent him to prison was his attack on the Prince Regent's debauchery rather than subversive activities. During the Greek War of Liberty, his periodical, the *Examiner*, paid a well-intentioned but vague tribute to the achievements of Ancient Greece: "We are all Greeks when we talk about nautical matters, arithmetic, theatres and dramas, poetry and philosophy, theology and cosmetics."[10] But the thought is not pursued with any consistency in anything that Hunt wrote.

He was a passionate lover of art. He was an amateur both in the etymological and the conventional sense of the word, and he had little theoretical background. But he had an impressive amount of intuition. He had a fine musical ear, and he was related to the painter Benjamin West, who opened his eyes to the beauties of the art of painting. Spenser was his favourite poet because his poetry is reminiscent of painting. He was good at spotting talents, even in very young artists, and he supported them to the best of his ability. He often draws parallels between the arts, and his emphasis throughout is on the elements of pleasure and entertainment conveyed by the works of art. But, of course, basically there is a didactic intention in most of what he wrote: he wanted to open "the eyes of the general reader" to the beauties of literature and painting. That is the *raison d'être* of his essay *What Is Poetry?* In fairness it should be added that his evaluation of other artists is completely free of the lapses into bad taste or even vulgarism that sometimes mar his polemical writing.

One of his really positive qualities was his frequent open admission of his own limitations. He realized that some of his translations were, in his own words, "worth very little", and more than once he admitted that he had revised passages of his earlier works because he "now" sees that they were not very successful. Such remarks are not mere coquetry, for Hunt was not a pushy man – he never boasted of his friendship with the big shots of the Romantic movement, and he never prided himself on having been the spiritual midwife of several of them.

II

Hunt's Relationship with Some of the Romantic Poets

Hunt's autobiography is not a document of absorbing interest. In large passages it is a piece of insipid writing, sentimentalizing the author and showing a peculiar sense of proportion in a man who devoted his life to writing in different literary genres, but who was also early aware that his political and poetical interests might be difficult to reconcile. The portrait that emerges is that of a well-intentioned, slightly self-centred elderly gentleman who expresses little or no interest in the theoretical basis of his profession. The autobiography is not a landmark in the intellectual history of mankind. On the other hand, it does not show Hunt as the evil genius who was responsible for Keats' lapses of taste – the standard criticism levelled against him.

But there is more to Hunt than meets the eye in his autobiography. It is a fact that there were aspects of his personality that interested, sometimes also attracted, men of letters who were of greater stature than himself.

Shelley
Shelley dedicated *The Cenci* to him with the following words: "Had I known a person more highly endowed than yourself with all that it becomes a man to possess, I had solicited for this work

the ornament of his name."[1] Hunt thanked him in a letter of 6th September 1819: (the dedication is) "one of the greatest honours as well as pleasures of which my nature is susceptible".[2] It is a fair guess that the incest motif of *The Cenci* prompted Hunt to write an epic with a similar theme, viz. *The Story of Rimini.*

The two men met in 1811, and they developed a life-long friendship. Hunt named his fourth son Percy Bysshe Shelley Hunt, and he defended Shelley in the *Examiner* on 10th October 1819: since it is impossible to refute Shelley's philosophical ideas, critics instead swoop on his private life. Hunt and Shelley corresponded eagerly while the latter was in Italy, and Hunt consistently braved the danger of standing up for the rebel Shelley. In his turn, Shelley admired Hunt for his unequivocal defence of Byron. At Hunt's imprisonment, Shelley was "boiling with indignation" at the "horrible injustice and tyranny" inflicted on a brave, good, and an intelligent man".[3] Several controversial works by Shelley were first printed in Hunt's periodical the *Examiner: Hymn to Intellectual Beauty* (1817) and *The Revolt of Islam* (1818). They shared political radicalism and a conviction that poetry had a mission to perform towards mankind.

Shelley attached great importance to Hunt's reviews of his poetry in the *Examiner* (letter to Hunt 1st May 1820),[4] and Hunt's reviews were honest, i.e. he gave generous praise where he felt it was due, but he did not shy away from making certain reservations: he praised *The Revolt of Islam* for its "depth of sentiment, grandeur of imagery, a versification remarkably sweet, various and noble" (The *Examiner*, 22nd February 1818), but blamed it for "obscurity" and "too great sameness of image". He acknowledges the greatness of *Adonais*, but adds that it is not calculated to be popular.

Hunt was deeply impressed by the cogency, as he saw it, of Shelley's philosophy: "We never lived with a man who gave so complete an idea of an ardent and principled aspirant in philosophy as Percy Shelley," he wrote in the *Examiner* on 10th October 1819 (No. 615). As could be expected, Hunt was enthusiastic about *Prometheus* (letter to Shelley, 23 August 1820), but in an

article in the *Examiner* on 16ᵗʰ June 1822 (No. 751) he character-
izes Shelley's poetry as being "often of a too abstract and
metaphysical cast".

In not a few cases, a modern reader would tend to agree with
Hunt's assessment of Shelley's poems, and many of his *obiter dicta*
on this and other subjects are – as was frequently the case with
Hunt – acute and sound. The remarkable thing is, however, that
Shelley never took umbrage at such strictures. On the contrary he
persistently maintained a conciliatory, almost reverential, attitude
towards Hunt, and when the latter was in financial straits, which
happened with great regularity, Shelley supported him with
unstinting generosity. And Shelley is not a little woolly when tack-
ling the thorny question of Hunt's alledgedly harmful influence
on Keats. *Hyperion* is a magnificent poem, but the rest of Keats'
poems are written in the bad style "which is becoming fashionable
among those who fancy that they are imitating Hunt and
Wordsworth" (letter to Mrs Hunt, 27ᵗʰ October 1820).[5]

It was Shelley who, at Byron's instigation, persuaded Hunt to
go to Italy in order to establish an editing partnership. Shelley
himself intended to be "only a sort of link between you and him"
(letter to Hunt, 26ᵗʰ August 1821). As is well known, the stay
became a catastrophe in every respect, but Hunt does not seem to
have born Shelley a grudge for it. On the contrary he says on several
occasions that Shelley is the only true friend he has had.

Byron

When Hunt was jailed in 1813 for attacking the scandalous
private life of the Prince Regent (Hunt's father was also a staunch
republican), Byron was attracted to this "imprisoned martyr". The
two men had met in 1804, and in the early stages of their acquain-
tance Hunt treated Byron with great reverence and referred to him
as "the noble lord".

Hunt defended Byron's private life and he also spoke in favour
of Lady Byron. He dedicated *The Story of Rimini* (1816) to Byron,
who, at this stage, extolled its virtues, but he also suggested some

amendments (e.g. of the mannerisms), which Hunt complied with. Hunt reciprocated by giving favourable reviews of Byron's poetry, and once more a modern reader must admire the perspicacity of Hunt's verdict: the strength of Byron's poetry resides in its passion and humour rather than in its imagery. Also he has no doubt that *Don Juan* will always be admired as a masterpiece.

However, later the relationship cooled considerably. The planned cooperation between the two at Pisa, where they started a periodical, *The Liberal*, became a short-lived affair. Byron became increasingly annoyed with his collaborator and attacked his poetry virulently – also *Rimini*, which he had earlier praised to the skies. In 1818 he wrote to Moore: "he (sc. Hunt) believes his trash of vulgar phrases tortured into compound barbarisms to be Old English".

Gradually, Byron took great pains to dissociate himself from Hunt. Critics found that Byron, who was an interesting person on the way to participating in the Greek War of Liberation, had degraded himself by his relationship with the vulgar Hunt. "There is no community of feeling between us," Hunt wrote in 1822. Things did not improve when, in the late 1820s, Hunt published *Lord Byron and Some of his Contemporaries*. The book was intended to be an honest portrait of, rather than a diatribe against, Byron, and Hunt defended himself by saying that he had not written anything he could not vouch for: Byron only wrote well when drunk, besides he was malicious and superstitious.[6] Still, some-what naïvely, Hunt was shocked by the violent reactions to the book, and the breach between Byron and himself never healed.

Keats

"We became friends, but I liked Shelley better", says Hunt about his relationship with Keats.[7] As early as in 1816, the year they first met, Hunt had shown his intuition as a talent-scout by calling Keats one of the promising young poets "who promise to help the new school to revive poetry", and in *Imagination and Fancy* he refers to Keats as "a born poet of the most poetical kind".[8]

Hunt supported and encouraged the young Keats: the latter's first published poem, *To Solitude*, was printed in Hunt's periodical the *Examiner*, *La Belle Dame sans Merci* appeared in the *Indicator*, and Hunt gave a discriminating review of Keats' *Poems* published in 1817. Characteristically he has some reservations on Keats' versification, but praises his feeling of intense beauty.[9] When Hunt assesses Keats' poetry, he makes light of what he considers weaknesses, but gives admiring comments on selected passages or the text as a whole. What appeals to Hunt is the musicality of the verse – sometimes goes into great detail on this point, evaluating the effect of individual sounds and rhymes – and the surprising effects of his images.

Keats admired Hunt's poetical zeal – probably *The Story of Rimini* was a source of inspiration for him – and for some time the two were very close, perhaps too close: Keats lived with the Hunts from May to August 1820. Hunt himself did not feel that he was patronizing the young poet, and he never boasted of having "discovered" and "marketed" Keats. One of Hunt's good qualities was his altruism where younger and unknown poets were concerned. However, they did have some brushes. Keats seems to have felt that Hunt was possessive and as early as in 1817 Keats writes, with a thinly veiled allusion to Hunt, that it is a great sin "to flatter oneself into the idea of being a great poet",[10] and in response to Hunt's somewhat lukewarm reception of *Endymion* he called Hunt's taste vulgar.

However, when the *Quarterly* and *Blackwood* levelled their devastating attack on Hunt as the leader of the Cockney School of Poetry and expressed surprise at Keats' connection with Hunt, Keats retorted angrily: "If there is (sc. any similarity between Hunt's poetry and mine), it is my natural way, and I have something in common with Hunt."[11] Keats was the protégé of Hunt and the younger and less experienced of the two. They lived in close contact for long periods, so it is unthinkable that a young and impressionable poet should not have been influenced by a man who, to a considerable extent, was his mentor. The intermittent turgidity of Keats' vocabulary bears the imprint of Hunt's linguistic idiosyncracies. Naturally, Hunt resented being called the leader of the Cockney School of Poetry, but he never saw himself as having had a bad influence on Keats. He was upset when he realized how ill Keats actually was, and he expressed genuine sorrow at the young poet's untimely death.

Coleridge

"A mighty intellect put upon a sensual body," said Hunt about Coleridge in his autobiography.[12] The two men never got on intimate terms: in the second of the *Lay Sermons* (1817), Coleridge had excoriated Hunt and other "living misleaders of the people". Many later critics have subscribed to Hunt's succinct characterization of Coleridge and his works: Coleridge was the most original thinker of the day, although perhaps too much influenced by German philosophy, and he reached sublime heights in his three poems *Christabel, Kubla Khan* and *The Ancient Mariner.*

Coleridge's distinction between imagination and fancy as well as his profound philosophical reflections were far beyond what Hunt could cope with, and Coleridge's predilection for defining his terms precisely was poles apart from Hunt's procedure. Hunt's summing up of the man and his achievement, "at the mercy of a discursive genius . . . willing to bring conviction and speculation together . . . satisfying nobody and concluding nothing",[13] contains more than a grain of truth.

Wordsworth

In *The Feast of Books* (1814), Hunt wrote a favourable review of *Poems in Two Volumes*, which Wordsworth had published in 1807. He showed more insight in what Wordsworth was getting at than several other reviewers ("he is at the head of a new and great age of poetry"), who had been very negative. But later he became less kind: he gave a reserved review of *Lyrical Ballads*: the authors place too great emphasis on nature, hence they "turn our thoughts away from society and men altogether"[14] (a curious evaluation). And he was decidedly unkind to Wordsworth and the Lake School in an article in the *Examiner* from 1818 (22nd February, No. 20):[15] the Lake School, "as they are called", have become just as dogmatic in their despair "as they used to be in their hope". And in the same periodical he writes on 9th May 1819: "The Poet of the Lake school always carries his egotism and saving knowledge about with him." Later, he was honest enough to admit that those words were written before he had acquainted himself properly with Wordsworth's poems. When he had actually read many of Wordsworth's poems, Hunt's evaluation became less severe. In the *Reflector* – another periodical of his – he pays tribute to Wordsworth's poetical genius, although he finds his choice of subjects peculiar.[16] However, that belated rehabilitation did not propitiate Wordsworth, who said in 1830: "Mr. Leigh Hunt is a coxcomb, was a coxcomb, and ever will be a coxcomb."[17]

Hazlitt

Hunt got on well with Hazlitt, who contributed many essays to several of his periodicals. Hunt was not blind to the fact that Hazlitt's articles conferred a certain standard on his publications, and everything goes to show that the reading public bought them not least because of Hazlitt's name.

Hunt's imprisonment in the years 1813–1815 was – particularly after the first year – more like keeping state than sitting behind bars: his family had free access to his cell, he was allowed to read and write at his own discretion; he wrote a masque called *The Descent of Liberty* plus several articles for the *Examiner,* and several of his friends and admirers – Henry Brougham, Charles Lamb, Jeremy Bentham, Maria Edgeworth and Hazlitt – paid regular visits to this "martyr of a good cause". At that time, Hunt was known as an ardent young reformer and an eloquent literary critic, and both Shelley and Byron felt a genuine admiration for him. And in his old age, when his financial situation was more than usually disastrous, a circle of Hunt's friends arranged benefit performances for him to help him out of his dire straits.

However, there is a reverse side to the coin: as time went on, his friends simply got tired of him. There were several reasons. It was not only the irresponsible way in which Hunt lived his life (and forced his wife and numerous children to live theirs). It was also that his "opaque speculations on the practical, legislative effects of imaginative literature proved more and more untenable", as Connell puts it.[18] As late as 1825, Hunt wrote in *Fiction and Matter-of-Fact*: "politics pushed further than common have been the cause of a new and greater impetus given to the sympathic imagination".[19] But that idea had long since proved totally erroneous.

When his friends visited him during his imprisonment, he was still a promising idealist, but the people who were in charge of the charity arrangement when Hunt was an old man simply acted out of pity. They had no confidence that Hunt's situation would improve (and they were right; incidentally, his father had also frequently felt the pressure of creditors), and they were not a little annoyed at his general insouciance and lack of real stature. They found that the charge levelled at him by the *Quarterly* as early as in 1809, viz. ignorance and vulgarity, was not wide of the mark.

And worse was to follow: the *Edinburgh Review* was an extremely influential periodical with an extensive circle of readers. In its heyday, 1812-1814, it became "a forum for the dissemination of ideas",[20] not least of a political kind, among the intelligentsia. Francis Jeffrey, the editor, was deeply engaged in politics, equally suspicious of radicalism and reaction. He ridiculed *Lyrical Ballads* because they targeted a mass audience which might be socially excited. The result might be a political upheaval, which would be disastrous in a period when England was at war with France. In October 1817, an anonymous contributor to the magazine launched a scathing attack on Hunt, whom the author characterized as "a man certainly of some talents, of extravagant pretensions, both in wit, poetry and politics, and withal of exquisitely bad taste, and extremely vulgar modes of thinking and manners in all respects". The author of that diatribe was John Gibson Lockhart, who shared Francis Jeffrey's fear of the decline of polite learning. Both men saw an intimate connection between the Cockney School of Poetry and the Cockney School of Politics.[21]

Most of Hunt's former friends fell away: Moore and Haydon came to dislike him; Hazlitt distanced himself gradually; Carlyle, whom Hunt rated highly for his erudition, considered him a superficial dilettante. Even Shelley, who remained a faithful friend until his death, had some discreet reservations. Thus it is characteristic that what he praises Hunt's poems for is their moral purity – not for their technical mastery or the forcefulness of their imagery. Byron's verdict epitomizes the prevailing attitude to Hunt: he despised him for his arrogance, his sense of being a martyr, and his unspeakable naïveté in the affairs of the world. And Harold Skimpole – a character in Dickens' *Bleak House* – was modelled on Hunt: an ageing person, carefree as a child, utterly devoid of any understanding of business affairs, moderately talented and with a musical ear, the father of a crowd of neglected children, and, in sum, totally incapable of asserting himself in life.

Hunt, who was unaware of any disagreement with Dickens, was genuinely taken aback and justifiably offended. Dickens energetically denied having had any malicious intention, but his disclaimer – he had only used "the light externals of character" – sounds feeble and convinced nobody.

III

Hunt's *What Is Poetry?*

The essay *What Is Poetry?* is an article in the book called *Imagination and Fancy, or Selections from the English Poets.* One reason why he wrote the essay may be Hunt's own genuine and spontaneous love of poetry: partly quoting Coleridge, he says, "poetry has been to me its own exceeding great reward".[1] He wanted to share his pleasure with his target group: "readers in general".

The essay opens with a definition of poetry and its purpose: Poetry is "the utterance of a passion for truth, beauty and power, embodying and illustrating its conceptions by imagination and fancy, and modulating its language on the principle of variety in uniformity . . . Its ends are pleasure and exaltation. Poetry stands between nature and convention, keeping alive among us the external and spiritual world."

Poetry is "an utterance", i.e. a verbal art. That statement may be an implicit criticism of Shelley's idea expressed in *A Defence of Poetry* that poetry is a term that covers all arts. Hunt separates poetry from the other arts when, on one of the first pages, he claims that poetry surpasses painting and music "in suggestiveness, range, and intellectual wealth".[2] At the same time, here and elsewhere, Hunt praises Spenser because his poetry shows a "remarkable relation to the art of the Painter".[3] The resources of poetry are extensive enough on account of "the variety of things to be expressed".[4] The poetical utterance is prompted by passion, which is defined in a footnote[5] as "suffering in a good sense", an echo of a statement by Coleridge in *Biographia Literaria* to the

effect that "there is no profession on earth which requires an atten-
tion so early, so long, or so unremitting as that of poetry; and
indeed as that of literary composition in general".[6]

From a later passage in Hunt's essay it can be inferred that the
passion is composed of beauty and love.[7] The passion, which must
be supposed to reside in the poet although Hunt says nothing
about how it came to be there in the first place or what inspires it,
is directed towards "truth, beauty and power". Already at this
stage we meet the terminological imprecision which is a charac-
teristic not only of much of this essay, but of virtually everything
that Hunt wrote. In decency it should be said that Hunt is not the
only author who is vague on definitions: all the Romantic poets
use words like *feeling, emotion, sentiment mood, idea, thought, imagi-
nation* and *fancy* almost indiscriminately.

Truth

Truth, Beauty and Pleasure are unequivocally positive terms to
Hunt. Truth remains undefined in the essay, but it is possible to
isolate some aspects of it as it is used in *What Is Poetry?* Later in
the essay he says that "Truth of any great kind whatsoever, makes
great writing", which means that there are several kinds of truth.
The "great kind" of truth includes the one to be found in a sweet
face or a bunch of violets,[8] as well as in Homer's epic and Gray's
Elegy[9.] (Gray was one of Hunt's favourite authors.) But the really
"great kind" of truth is "truth of feeling"; a mimetic representa-
tion of the objects of *natura naturata* is not Hunt's prime concern.

Truth, in Hunt's perception, has an effect of permanence; it is
contrasted with "the fleeting and the false".[10] Without truth the
impression (sc. conveyed by a poem) would be false and defective.[11]
Truth is achieved by the poet as well as his readers: on the one hand
it signifies truthfulness in the rendering of the poet's passion:
"Truth of every kind belongs to him provided it can bud into any
kind of beauty, or is capable of being illustrated and impressed by
the poetic faculty."[12] On the other hand, truth is arrived at by a

kind of consensus among readers: "the consent and delight of poetic readers" makes poetry true.[13] A modern reader response critic would nod approval.

Hunt pays tribute to Ariosto for giving "a constant harmonious sense of truth and beauty".[14] In his *Ode on a Grecian Urn* Keats had identified truth and beauty, and also to Hunt — who wrote after the publication of Keats' poem — the two are intimately connected. He cites English ballads and romances as examples of the identification of them.[15]

Hunt also addresses the issue that has preoccupied poets and theorists from Plato and onwards, and which was to acquire added significance with the advent of Positivism later in the 19th century, viz. the never resolved conflict between the truth of science and the truth of poetry. Hunt is at pains to ascribe "traditional" truth value to poetical statements: poetical "perceptions" are true "by the fact of their existence", which means that, perhaps unwittingly, Hunt applies the yardstick of science. The similarity is pursued: science, like poetry, originates in feeling, and what poets claim in their "remotest imaginations" may often be found to have the closest connection with matters of fact; perhaps it might always be so "if the subtlety of our perceptions were a match for the cause of them".[16] In other words, the respective statements of science and poetry may frequently be quasi-identical, only our comprehension is too limited to grasp it. Hunt quotes Bacon in support of his statement at this stage: "the same fact of Nature" may be seen "treading different paths".[17]

However, at the present stage of our intellectual development there may be similarity, but never dove-tailing: the truth of poetry is at a higher level than that of science: "Poetry begins where matter of fact or science ceases to be merely such, and to exhibit a further truth."[18] Poetry takes over where science has to stop, so to speak, because poetry has a connection "with the world of emotion" and is able to produce "imaginative pleasure".[19] Hunt quotes with approval what he takes to be Milton's defence of poetry: in comparison with science, poetry is simple, sensuous, and passionate, and he construes the statement as follows. "simple" means "unperplexed and self-evident"; "sensuous" means "general and full of imagery"; "passionate" means "excited and enthusiastic".[20] Science is limited in that perception is "the only final proof" of what it can demonstrate. However, feeling is the "earliest" teacher, hence the more reliable one. To Hunt, poetic truth is not the opposite of factual truth, but it supplements and enriches the latter thanks to the imagination's play with words.

Hunt's opinion is reminiscent of Wordsworth's statement to the effect that "poetry is the breath and spirit of all knowledge; it is the impassioned expression which is in the countenance of all science".[21] Shelley had called poetry "that which comprehends all science, and that to which all science must be referred".[22]

Beauty

Beauty is an undefined, but ultimate plus value that, like the spirit of God, moves upon the face of Hunt's texts dealing with aesthetics. Even if the term is infrequently used in this text, it is implicitly present throughout, for example in his exemplifications, as the standard of reference and goal to be achieved. When the word does occur, its fundamental significance is made evident: it is held to convey the highest form of pleasure, and, together with love, it is "the parent of poetry".[23] Besides, in accordance with Hunt's emphasis on the linguistic aspect of poetry, beauty is "associated with sound",[24] which, to Hunt, is nearly synonymous with versification.

Power

Power is a concept used by Hunt and other Romantic authors in theories of poetry. It is an appropriate designation for the two-way traffic that is operative in a poem: on the one hand the force that impels the inspired poet, on the other the impact that the finished product makes on the reader. In his Preface,[25] Wordsworth talks about a man who feels pleasure at his own passions and volitions and who enjoys seeing them "as manifested in the goings on of the universe". Such a man has developed a greater readiness and power in expressing what he thinks and feels, particularly the thoughts that arise in him "without immediate external excitement". Power, then, is one of the attributes of the creative mind, it demands and facilitates expression. What we meet here is the well-known Romantic concept of harmony – the great unity between man and the outside world.

Imagination and Fancy

The "conceptions" of the poet's passion, i.e. his inspiration, whose source is left unmentioned, are verbalized by "imagination and fancy", which seem to be two different approaches to the creation of poetry as well as being the distinguishing qualities of the finished poems. In the preface to the essay, we read that poetry changes "from imagination to fancy through all their degrees".[26]

Before Coleridge, the two words imagination and fancy had not been rigidly separated. Thus, Addison named one of his works *Pleasures of the Imagination or Fancy (which I shall use promiscuously).* But Coleridge established a qualitative distinction between the two: he conceived of "primary imagination" as a parallel, on the human level, to "the eternal act of creation in the divine mind". The divine overtones are unmistakable. "Secondary imagination" was different in degree, but not in kind: "at all events it struggles to idealize and unify".[27] It is something that a human being can achieve. The distinction, then, covers a much larger area than poetry.

Fancy is inferior to imagination because "it must receive all its materials ready made from the law of association".[28] Coleridge devoted a considerable amount of energy in to refuting Hartley's law of association, and he needed a term that would characterize the mental process underlying that law. His philosophical distinction proved eminently applicable to the realm of poetic creation and poetic achievement, and it established a paradigm that has been valid to this day: fancy is inferior to imagination because it produces poetry that is inferior to the products of imagination.

In a passage in *What Is Poetry?* Hunt gives vent to some impatience with the two terms: they were "formerly identical or used as such; and neither is the best that might be found".[29] "Some new term is wanting to express the more spiritual sympathies of what is called Imagination."[30] However, Hunt does not suggest a solution, nor does he pursue his criticism. He never put the Coleridgean distinction to any theoretical use. Yet it is as if Coleridge's terms provide a frame which determines his discussion of poetry. He thanks "Coleridge and his fellows for having re-awakened true inspiration",[31] but he gives the pair a less precise extension than did Coleridge. In fact, he treats imagination as a kind of poetical panacea. It is important to note that to Hunt imagination and fancy are also linguistic entities, which is not surprising considering his emphasis on versification, metre and rhyme as essential ingredients of poetry.

Hunt uses the two terms as instruments to separate the wheat from the chaff: they are qualitative designations of categories of poetry, imagination ranking higher than fancy (as it did to Coleridge), "which is a lighter play of imagination, or the feeling of analogy coming short of seriousness in order hat it may laugh with what it loves, and show how it can decorate it with fairy ornament".[32] Fancy, in Hunt's idiolect, is a carefree and inferior, but still inherently valuable, variant of imagination. It is even able to evoke laughter: "Imagination belongs to Tragedy, or the serious muse; Fancy to the comic."[33] Fancy appealed to a man of Hunt's genial disposition; numerous passages in Hunt's oeuvre testify to his positive attitude to the concept. The reference in the quotation above to "analogy" shows that Hunt was familiar with Coleridge's discussion of the theory of association.

In *What Is Poetry?* the term imagination is made to serve multifarious functions. In the first paragraph of the essay, poetry embodies and illustrates the impressions by "imagination, or images of the objects of which it treats".[34] In this context, imagination seems to refer to the (poet's) power of creating images, i.e. a conventional meaning of the word.

Later in the essay,[35] Hunt lists kinds and degrees of imagination: "1) that which presents to the mind any object or circumstances in everyday life; 2) that which presents real, but not everyday circumstances; 3) that which combines character and events directly imitated from real life, with imitative realities of its own invention; 4) that which conjures up things and events not to be found in nature; 5) that which, in order to illustrate or aggravate one image introduces another . . . .sometimes in simile . . . sometimes in metaphor; 6) that which reverses this process, and makes a variety of circumstances take colour from one (e.g. the flowers and flocks are made to sympathize with a man's death); 7) that which, by a single expression, apparently of the vaguest kind, not only meets but surpasses in its effects the extremest force of the most particular description."

As will be seen, it is a mixed bag, poles apart from Coleridge's cogent, almost mathematical definition, but also a highly idiosyncratic collection. Some of the categories – (1), (2), and (3) – refer to sources of inspiration: everyday life supplemented with "imitative realities of its own invention". The emphasis is on the creative force – the poet's share is only implied, unlike the active part that is attributed to him, in, for example, Wordsworth's Preface.

The seven categories range from the down-to-earth to the fantastical ("things and events not to be found in nature" (4)). Hunt does not tell his readers how the categories can be made to square. Some refer to the sources of inspiration, others to the power of expression. No. 5 refers to a linguistic unit, a simile or a metaphor, which is much like No. 7: the well-chosen and striking expression. No. 6 makes imagination almost synonymous with the pathetic fallacy. The subdivision is not pursued with any kind of consistency in the rest of the essay, and Fancy is never given the same detailed treatment as imagination.

Hunt chimes in with Shelley's homage to imagination: it is "the great instrument of moral good"[36] (even if that capacity is not included in the listing given above), so, in some unexplained way, imagination can also serve an ethical purpose. Poetry is "imaginative passion", he says,[37] and in his account "imaginary creatures" rub shoulders with "metaphor", which, with some justification, is called "the common coin of discourse",[38] and with imaginary creatures from literature, e.g. Ariel and Caliban.[39] Imagination teems with action and character: it is one of the epic poet's resources.

Imagination is also concerned with the supernatural, and in that area the poet must not "humanize weakly or mistakenly"; if he does so, he risks forgetting "to be true to the supernatural itself",[40] and in that case he also forsakes nature: "for it will be wanting to be supernatural, as Nature would have made it, working in a supernatural direction."[41] What this somewhat cryptic statement seems to mean is that even supernatural phenomena and creatures should be kept well within the bounds of nature: the poet "takes the world with him" "by making Nature his companion".[42] Invented characters should be brought into "regions of truth and likelihood".[43]

Imagination is the metaphor-creating power, hence intimately connected with expression, for the opposite of imagination shows itself as "pure absence of ideas, in commonplaces and, above all, in conventional metaphor, or such images and their phraseology as have become the common property of discourse and writing".[44] So, a written presentation devoid of imagination becomes flat and makes use of dead metaphors.

Imagination is the supreme value in Hunt's scale. He makes it a kind of Jack-of-all-trades, allowing it even to encroach on territory he himself assigns to Fancy: both of them are concerned with analogies. Imagination is "the feeling of the subtlest and most affecting analogies, the perception of sympathies in the nature of things, or in their popular attributes".[45] Imagination, then, enables us to gain true insight into the way "things" are connected. It is understandable, therefore, that Hunt should call for a more comprehensive generic term. "The term imagination is too confined," he says,[46] but he offers no alternative linguistic suggestion and drops the idea almost immediately. To Hunt, imagination is a given, a quality that is the prerequisite of the production of good poetry.

He makes it an umbrella term to cover some aspects not usually included under that heading, e.g. morals. That explains his dissatisfaction with the conventional term, but it would be difficult, not to say impossible, to think of a designation that would straddle all the aspects he subsumes under the heading of imagination and its derivatives.

Whereas Coleridge informed his readers about what imagination *was* ("the primary IMAGINATION I hold to be . . . " . . . "the secondary imagination I consider as . . . "), to Hunt imagination is an unspecified "that which", i.e. a factor that *does* several things: presents, introduces, reverses, conjures up. As always, Hunt chooses a pragmatic rather than a theoretical approach. That may be ascribed to inability or unwillingness on Hunt's part to dig deeper, but a kinder interpretation might cite it as an instance of consideration for his target group, "the general reader", who would probably benefit more from Hunt's examples with the purple patches italicized. Also, the poet and his activity are left entirely out of consideration – what matters is the result, neither the origin nor the process. Accordingly, Hunt treats imagination partly as an instrument whereas to Coleridge it had been a mental faculty.

Feeling and Thought

Feeling is a word that always appears in a positive context in *What Is Poetry?* It is closely allied to imagination – and the treatment of it is equally elusive.

In one passage, feeling is the raw material of imagination ("Imagination is all feeling"),[47] a statement that is reminiscent of Wordsworth's "All good poetry is the spontaneous overflow of powerful feelings".[48] Hunt uses the generic singular (feeling), and he has no specific emotion – such as love, grief or patriotism – in mind. Rather, feeling refers to a moment or state of heightened sensibility in a poet, and thus comes very close to being synonymous with inspiration.

Feeling and one function of imagination make up a pair analogous to the classical diptych *inventio-dispositio*, feeling being the starting-point and imagination the arrangement. Feeling is necessary to the perception, and imagination to the licking into shape, "even of matters of fact". Feeling also teaches or advises the poet to make the appropriate choices, to find or think of (which is the etymological meaning of invent) a solution; without it, there is "a want of delicacy and distinction". Imagination, in its turn, ensures the felicitous formulation; without it, "there is no true embodiment".[49]

According to Wordsworth, poems of any value have always been written "by a man who, being possessed of more than usual organic sensibility, had also thought long and deeply".[50] Apparently he saw no conflict between that thinking activity and the spontaneous overflow. In one passage, Hunt relegates thought to an inferior position because "thought by itself makes no poet at all, for the mere conclusions of understanding can at best be only so many intellectual matters of fact".[51] Obviously he had not understood the part played by reason in the theoretical reflections of the Romantic poets.

Feeling stands a far better poetical chance than thought because it "seldom makes the blunders that thought does",[52] and Hunt goes so far as to warn young poets against "that tendency to an accumulation and ostentation of *thought*" (his italics).[53] Even Shakespeare must yield to Homer because there is too much of "that incessant activity of thought" in his dramas.[54]

However, in a later passage, thought is somewhat rehabilitated: "Prosaicalness is the consequence of weak thought."[55] The implication is that poetry is the true medium for great thoughts, with the proviso, however, that "thought" alone cannot create great poetry. Thought should know its place: it is a necessary but not sufficient condition in the creative process.

Fancy

Right from the outset, fancy is defined as a lighter play of the imagination,[56] and that attitude is maintained throughout the essay: fancy is "a younger sister of Imagination, without the other's weight of thought and feeling".[57] It is "sporting with their (sc. the things') resemblances, real or supposed, and with airy and fantastical creations".[58] Fancy's connection with association is discernible here.

Fancy is more down-to-earth than imagination: it "has rarely that freedom from visibility which is one of the highest privileges of imagination".[59] Whereas imagination can create awe-inspiring figures – it is "busied with spiritual affinities and the mysteries of the universe"[60] – fancy is more concrete, but also less profound: "the genius of fairies, of gallantries, of fashions; of whatever is quaint and light, showy and capricious".[61]

The difference between imagination and fancy is one of seriousness and literary value, in the poet's oeuvre as well as in individual works and passages. "In the greatest poets, Fancy and Imagination go hand in hand, to the minor poets, fancy is the greater favourite."[62] Hunt illustrates his point by quoting italicized passages exemplifying imagination from Shakespeare's *Troilus and Cressida*, and passages illustrating fancy from *Love's Labour's Lost*. In the latter example he sees "a combination of images not in their nature connected, or brought together by the feeling, but by the will and pleasure".[63] The analogies that Fancy finds, then, are not "naturally" given, but imposed from outside. Coleridge had voiced a similar opinion in *Biographia Literaria*: fancy is a mode of memory "blended with and modified by that empirical phenomenon of the will, which we express by the word choice", and he claimed that "the Fancy must receive all its materials ready made from the law of association".[64]

Hunt's examples are intended to prove his point: Spenser has more fancy than imagination, Milton has more imagination than fancy, Pope has hardly any imagination, but a considerable amount of fancy – and Shakespeare has the two in equal perfection.

Characteristically, in a hierarchical listing of what gifts make the greatest poets, fancy only comes in fourth. But, generally speaking, Hunt does not seem to have found the profundity of the Coleridgean distinction useful. Another noteworthy feature is that the examples Hunt quotes to illustrate the difference do not always carry conviction because the distinction seems to be imposed idiosyncratically: some of his examples might actually be said to work both ways.

Language

In Hunt's introductory definition, poetry is said to modulate "its language on the principle of variety in uniformity".[65] In the light of the content of *What Is Poetry?* and of Hunt's opinions as expressed elsewhere in his writings, the statement is remarkable for its brevity as well as for its focus.

It is obvious from the whole essay that language is *the* distinguishing feature of poetry, language in a restricted sense of the word, that is. The essay almost exclusively focuses on versification, rhyme and rhythm at the expense of vocabulary. Surprisingly, there are no references to Hunt's own poetical practice or his often highly idiosyncratic vocabulary. He was notorious for using rare or obsolete words (*swaling*), making words change their conventional class (*core* as a verb), producing strange results by a generous sprinkling of –ly endings (*lightsomely*), and by creating unusual concatenations (*side-long pillowed meekness*). That is the more remarkable because, in connection with *The Story of Rimini*, he had complained that "modern poetry" is marred by using "sophisticated phrases of *written* language instead of the *spoken* language of real feeling".[66] Even well-intentioned friends and positive reviewers had some reservations with regard to Hunt's use of language in his poetry although they were often euphemistically formulated.

In the preface to *The Story of Rimini* Hunt advocated "a free and idiomatic use of language", and poets were advised to use "a natural existing language, omitting of course *mere* vulgarisms and fugitive phrases, which are the cant of ordinary discourse"[67] (his italics). The poem itself effectively contradicted that manifesto. It is a paradox that Hunt, who elsewhere spoke up eagerly against conventional "poetic diction" actually contributed heavily to creating one of his own. At least he must have been convinced that poetry required a particular idiom.

He undercuts his own passing, but potentially rewarding, reference to metaphor, "the common coin of discourse",[68] by applying the term metaphor to imaginary creatures from literature, such as Ariel and Caliban And he immediately flies off at a tangent by starting to talk about Spenser, Ariosto, Hobbes and Chaucer, and to describe their characteristics and peculiarities.

It is characteristic of Hunt's conception that the genuine poet shows his mastery in his verbalizations. A prominent place is awarded to what Hunt calls "expression". "The quickest and the subtlest test of the possession of the essence (sc. of poetry) is expression."[69] And in Hunt's idiolect, expression is virtually synonymous with versification. *What Is Poetry?* is a loving tribute to verse and versification. It is the fitness or unfitness for *song* (Hunt's italics) or "metrical excitement" that "make all the difference between a poetical and a prosaical subject".[70] Some subjects lend themselves more immediately than others to poetical treatment, it seems. It is one of the few passages where Hunt talks about the subject of poetry; but it is made clear that form rather than subject is the determining factor.

Verse is the basic ingredient and supporting pillar of poetry. It is required in poetry for "the perfection of poetical spirit"[71] – again the idea that true poetry is versified (but, as we shall see, not necessarily rhymed) language. A true poet will feel "desire" and "necessity" to "write in verse". "What great poet ever wrote his poems in prose, or where is a good prose poem, of any length, to be found?"[72] Hunt instances the Bible, which in its original language was written in verse.[73] "Verse is the final proof to the poet that his mastery over his art is complete."[74] There is an intimate connection between versification and the quality of poetry: "I know of no very fine versification unaccompanied with fine poetry; no poetry of a mean order accompanied with verse of the highest."[75] Here we have another of Hunt's sweeping generalizations that a modern reader would like to see exemplified. It is also one of the rare sidelong glances at content – without using the word, it is true.

Poet and verse have a "reciprocal bond", "they are lovers playfully challenging each other's rule, and delighted equally to rule and obey".[76] To the inspired poet, verse is equivalent to a mental force. It is held to spring form "the same enthusiasm as the rest of his impulses, and is necessary to their satisfaction and effect".[77] It has a will-power of its own, and it satisfies some deep-rooted needs in the privileged poet. The creation of verse is spontaneous and irresistible, it is "the answer of form to his (sc. the poet's) spirit".[78] The highest compliment that can be paid to verse is that a mystic communion is held to exist between it and the poet's soul.

"Every poet, then, is a versifier, every fine poet is an excellent one, and he is the best whose verse exhibits the greatest amount of strength, sweetness, straightforwardness, unsuperfluousness, *variety* and *one-ness*" (his italics).[79] Again Hunt focuses not on content, vocabulary, use of metaphor, felicitous phrasing, or the like, but on the construction of the verse of the poem. The qualities of versification that he requires are subjective, but only arbitrary to the extent that Hunt's extensive reading permits him to find appropriate illustrations of the individual verse qualities. The result is that the abstract terms come to be less vague than they would at first glance seem to be, and the reader is actually able to see what Hunt is getting at. Typically, as Hunt sees it, the overall aim of poetry is to convey pleasure.

Strength is primarily a linguistic factor. It manifests itself "in the number and force of marked syllables",[80] not, as might have been expected, in the clarity or depth of the poet's thinking. That point is tackled indirectly because in a later passage,[81] weakness, the opposite of strength, "generally accompanies prosaicalness, and is the consequence of weak thoughts." Hunt obviously has a point here, for flabby thinking rarely produces sublime poetry. Strength, in Hunt's idiolect, is purely a matter of rhythm. Thus *"straightforwardness"* means "the flow of words in their natural order, which is not equivalent to "mere prose", but for example the avoidance of inversion for the sake of the rhymes.[82] It does not refer to the accessibility of the content. *"Superfluousness"*, too, is a matter of words: it simply means using too many words. "What hope can remain for wordy mediocrity?"[83] Superfluousness is permissible in cases of "overflowing animal spirits", which would seem to be a pretty wide margin. Curiously, in this case Hunt's example is the Elizabethan dramatists Beaumont and Fletcher. An exemption can also be granted to the few poets who demonstrate "a genius of luxury", as is the case with one of Hunt's great favourites, viz. Spenser. But apart from that, "there is no worse sign (sc. than superfluousness) for a poet altogether, except pure barrenness".[84]

A malicious reader might point to the fact that Hunt uses an impressive array of words to prove the harmfulness of superfluousness. Also, it would be misleading to characterize the style of his works in general as brief or terse.

"Sweetness" is, on the surface, a bland criterion; to Hunt it has something to do with the poet's use of vowels and consonants[85] – but there is more to it than that: sweetness is achieved by the poet using "the principle of variety in uniformity", which was mentioned in his introductory definition. It is the classical *concordia discors* idea,[86] which was left largely unmentioned by Wordsworth, Shelley and Coleridge, but which is a fundamental criterion to Hunt. Uniformity is a kind of basis material, variety an indispensable ingredient or superstructure. The "main secrets" of sweetness are a smooth progression between "variety and sameness",[87] i.e. sweetness is the result of a Hegelian dialectical progression. "One-ness of impression will be diversely produced."[88] Hunt finds the quality in the poetical works of

Coleridge and Shelley, and, characteristically, Spenser is full of it. Where greater poets have sweetness, lesser ones have smoothness, which is inferior because it is not the outcome of a tension between opposites.

"*One-ness*" means metrical and moral consistency, i.e. it refers to form as well as to content. The latter concept plays a decidedly minor role in the essay. *Variety* means "every pertinent diversity of tone and rhythm".[89] Unexpected locations of the accent increase the strength of verse.[90] Both uniformity and variety are necessary, but Hunt devotes more space to variety and speaks more warmly about it than about its opposite number. Variety holds three trump cards: it makes for a more pithy expression, and, as we have seen, expression was one of the supporting pillars of Hunts' theory of poetry; secondly, it is a significant rhythmical factor; and, thirdly, it is conducive to the reader's pleasure by stopping him being bored.

By variety, Hunt means "Whatever can be done for the prevention of monotony, by diversity of stops and cadences, distribution of emphasis, and the retardation and acceleration of time; for the whole secret of versification is a musical secret."[91] Accordingly, it is not enough for the poet to know "all feet and numbers and accent and quantity". It is a matter of " . . . the beautiful in poetical passion, accompanied by musical".[92] Hunt proceeds to illustrate his point by criticizing the "see-saw" of Pope's versification in *The Rape of the Lock*,[93] but he does admit that Pope is "exquisite in his with and fancy".[94] So Pope had uniformity (again it is not difficult to see what Hunt is driving at), but lacked the ingredient of it which would have raised his work to a higher level, viz. variety.

Metre is central to Hunt's idea of what poetry is made up of because it is the conveyor of rhythm. *What Is Poetry?* contains some references to the couplet (e.g. as used by Pope), and a compliment to Coleridge for his ingenious use of the octosyllabic: he realized that it was not a matter of the number of syllables, but rather of "the *beat of the form* into which you might get as many syllables as you could".[95] Hunt cites *Christabel* and praises it because, in that poem, versification becomes part of the sentiment. Altogether, in Hunt's evaluation of the poem, his concern with variety in uniformity is clearly discernible. Posterity agrees with him: the strength of *Kubla Khan* resides not in the mechanical observance of a metrical pattern, but in the poet's discriminate use, in each line, of free and rhythm-creating syllables.

Rhyme is a significant component of poetry, not as a mechanical exercise, but because of the effects of surprise and novelty it can add to the beauty of a poem. Again variety is the key word: a writer ought to know how "to vary it, to give it novelty . . . to divide it (when not in couplets) at the proper intervals . . . .and to make it in comic poetry, a new and surprising addition to the jest".[96] Rhyme should not be a straitjacket on the poem, but an integrated element, contributing smoothly to the total effect. As a matter of fact, rhyme is "one of the musical beauties of verse for all poetry but epic and dramatic . . . ".[97] And yet Hunt calls Molière "the most perfect master of rhyme" besides being "the greatest writer of comedy the world has ever seen".[98] As will have appeared, this is not the only case showing some discrepancy between Hunt's theoretical statements and his exemplification.

The Purpose of Poetry

It may seem peculiar, in an essay about what poetry is, to include reflections on what it does and should do. But here Hunt follows venerable precedents: in his *Poetics*, Aristotle said that "tragedy . . . should imitate such actions as excite terror and pity (this being the peculiar property of the tragic imitation",[99] and Horace said in *Ars poetica* that the poet's wish was either to delight or to instruct: "aut prodesse volunt aut delectare poetae".[100]

Hunt emphasizes the *delectare* aspect – the *prodesse* was less important for his purpose, which was not to defend poetry e.g. against attacks of immorality.

Pleasure is one of the most frequently occurring words in Hunt's oeuvre. In his theatrical reviews, for example, he largely evaluates plays according to the amount of pleasure they give him. And pleasure means to Hunt sheer hedonism. It is not an intellectual thrill, the feeling that accompanies greater understanding or deeper insight.

Yet a discreet *prodesse* is always implicit in his reflections on poetry. A slight moral ingredient is perceptible in one of the words Hunt uses in the opening paragraph of his essay, viz. exaltation. The word may be used to describe a moral uplift, and in that case poetry may be said to be emotionally and ethically edifying. Hunt wanted his essay to be a sort of poetical vademecum for "the general reader". Hence the discreet element of instruction. The same path had been trodden by Shelley: that element is the pivot of his *Defence of Poetry.*

Nature vs. Convention

As early as in the first paragraph of *What Is Poetry?*, poetry is represented as an intermediary between "nature" and "convention".

On the linguistic level, the first member of the pair refers to what the poet's mind is grappling with when it is at the stage of gestation. The second points to the conventional, i.e. ordinary and non-poetical, use of language. The language of poetry is a huge storehouse: "The variety of things to be expressed shows the variety of its resources."[101]

Hunt's formula also shows that, like Coleridge, he distances himself from Wordsworth's statement in the Preface that "there neither is, nor can be, any *essential* difference between the language of prose and metrical composition".[102] A little earlier in the Preface Wordsworth had said that "The language of a large part of every good poem must necessarily, especially with reference to the metre, in no respect differ from that of good prose."[103]

That is poles apart from Hunt's opinion. To him, versification and metre – i.e. rhythm – were the hallmarks of poetry and two of the ingredients that made poetry clearly distinguishable from prose. Hunt was not at all concerned with the relationship between the language of poetry and that of prose. Even if he did not advocate any kind of poetic diction, he had no doubt that poetry had a language of its own. His own poetry furnishes abundant illustration of that thesis.

On the intellectual or spiritual level, poetry is held by Hunt to stand between the way we usually perceive things (convention), and what they are really like (nature). Thus poetry is instrumental in bringing about a better understanding of the sublunary world as well as what lies beyond or above it. It was a familiar Romantic view that the strength of poetry lies not least in its ability to convey fresh insight. As Shelley put it (quoted by Hunt towards the end of his essay), "poetry lifts the veil from the hidden beauty of the world and makes unfamiliar objects as if they were not new".[104]

That idea was taken up by later poets. In the beginning of the 20th century, the Imagists and T. E. Hulme questioned the Positivists' claim to be able to give the only truthful picture of reality. To them, reality might just as well be understood intuitively, viz. in the insight conveyed by the striking poetical image.[105]

Again, a didactic purpose is discreetly hinted: poetry teaches us to enjoy both the material and the spiritual world; it straddles two worlds, being, as Hunt formulates it early in the essay, "the greatest proof to man of the pleasure to be found in all things, and of the probable riches of infinitude".[106]

The Poet

According to Wordsworth, the poet is "a man speaking to men",[107] but his subsequent listing of the characteristics of a poet shows that he is a "richly endowed man": he must possess "sensibility, enthusiasm, tenderness, knowledge, a compulsive soul", "more than are supposed to be common among mankind".[108] The qualities fit in nicely with what might be called Wordsworth's poetical philosophy.

As we have seen, Hunt sees a kind of reciprocity between the poet and his poetry: "Verse is the answer of form to his spirit."[109] Accordingly, most of the qualities he requires of the poet are some that also characterize successful poetry: thought, feeling, expression, imagination, action, character and continuity, "all in the largest amount and highest degree". Most of those characteristics are elaborated as the essay goes along, and two of them, viz. expression and imagination are the fulcra of Hunt's argumentation. "Action" and "character" explain Hunt's ranking, later in the essay, of the epic as the highest "class of poetry".[110]

The noteworthy thing is that the poet tends to disappear in *What Is Poetry?* Thus, in his subdivision of the concept of imagination, the agent seems to be of decidedly inferior interest. For instance item 3 talks about invention, but does not see it as a talent in the poet; item 5 elaborates on "one image", but we hear nothing about who is responsible for the creation of the image. The other items all start with "that which" – a thing or phenomenon, not a human being. The essay largely ignores the poet's role as creator.

Only towards the end is the poet pulled on stage again: his distinguishing feature is "that power of undervaluing nothing, and no attainments different from his own".[111] However, those words are not so much a humanistic manifesto as a kow-tow to the incipient onrush of technological inventions. For Hunt goes on to say that the poet's imagination enables him to acknowledge useful modern phenomena like railways and steam engines, and to realize that they can bring an "incalculable amount of good and knowledge, and refinement and mutual consideration".[112]

In those lines, Hunt anticipates what was to become science's trump card later in the 19th century: the fact that its results actually gave people better living conditions. However, Hunt adds that utility must not be allowed to oust "the noblest necessities of the human mind", and, as Bacon has pointed out, poetry is essential for the satisfaction of the human mind. With his tongue in his cheek Hunt adds that Bacon was, if anything, a scientist.

Other Subjects

These "other subjects" are really nothing but brief digressions. Some demands are made on the reader: nobody can become a good reader without sharing the poet's interest and affection, be it the firmament or the daisy[113] – an echo of Coleridge's "willing suspension of disbelief". And the question of telling a good poem from a bad one is made speciously simple: the point is to read many good poets very attentively. That is of course begging the question, for Hunt does not give the reader any clue as to how to find a good poet in the first place.

In what can be characterized as a brief aside, Hunt adopts the Neo-classical hierarchization of literary genres. He calls the epic the "highest class of poetry" because it "includes the drama, with narration besides; or the speaking and action of the characters, with speaking of the poet himself".[114] The remark seems to be prompted by a sudden inspiration, and the idea is dropped almost immediately.

IV

A Critique of
What Is Poetry?

The context of the essay is the book called *Imagination and Fancy*, which is not a theoretical discussion, but *"Selections from the English Poets . . . with Markings of the best Passages"*. The "critical notices" that Hunt promises at the beginning are mostly scattered remarks of a subjective and un-theoretical kind. The book is an annotated anthology which, according to the Preface, will deal with "the nature and requirements of poetry". That promise is not kept in the essay.

The full title of the essay is *"An Answer to the Question: What is Poetry"*. The question was presumed to be asked by "the general reader", an anonymous and nondescript category of people who are the target group of virtually all that Hunt wrote. The purpose is gently didactic – an attempt to isolate the essence of poetry and to open the readers' eyes to the beauties of it by means of an abundance of examples rather than strict theorizing.

It is not a polemical piece of writing. Nor is it a defence of poetry (in the vein of Shelley) or an attempt to propagate a specific theory (as Wordsworth did in the Preface to the Second Edition of *Lyrical Ballads*). And it is poles apart from the philosophical and speculative approach that Coleridge adopted in *Biographia Literaria*. It is not a follow-up on, or a criticism of, those three works – they are not mentioned in *What is Poetry?* Nor is it an attempt at marketing his own work. The purpose is, as Hunt himself expressed it elsewhere in an article about Milton, "to give the reader no perplexity except to know what to admire most". And Hunt took care to italicize the passages in his selections that he found most worthy of admiration.

Form

From the beginning, the essay attempts a systematic approach: it opens with a definition of what poetry is, followed by a statement of its purpose. After that, Hunt proceeds to describe the qualities of the poet, and he makes a subdivision of imagination. However, that subdivision, which is, at best, highly idiosyncratic, is not at all maintained in the rest of the essay, which is characterized by a loose and desultory structure. The style is associational, and though Hunt now and then tries to explain in what the beauty of his italicized passages consists, he obviously finds it difficult to stick to his subject. Thus, he ends his essay with an irrelevant tribute to the usefulness of railways. Also, one might ask what is the *raison d'être* of his hierarchization of the different categories of poetry.

What Is Poetry? peters out in largely irrelevant digressions, and it does not make up a whole or give the reader an impression of unity. It just ends where it ends. The essay remains a torso, a series of illustrations that are not arranged according to any clear chronological or thematic plan. However, that is not tantamount to saying that the essay is devoid of interest.

Content

The emphasis is not on theory, but on practice. The strength of it is Hunt's genuine, almost contagious, enthusiasm for poetry. His selections are subjective, but actually most of his examples and opinions of them would hold water in the 21st century. He is a true connoisseur in his talent of separating the wheat from the chaff. His illustrative examples are nearly always sound and often very acute. He draws on many sources and is generous in his choices, which are evidence of his extensive reading: several centuries are represented, but he does not quote examples from his own poems. His examples are often taken from poets that were little known or downright unpopular with his contemporaries. However, that is a factor that contributes to the relevance of the essay. It is imaginable that what Hunt wanted to show was that poetry written in other ages than the Romantic was *also* valuable and rewarding. That means that *What Is Poetry?* is not only more reader-friendly than the theoretical speculations of Wordsworth, Coleridge and Shelley, but also that his work heralded, in a modest way, a break-away from the Romantic paradigm of what could be classified, and accepted, as good poetry. Thus, consciously or unconsciously, he contributes to widening the concept of "good poetry". It should be borne in mind that the essay was published in 1825, i.e. at a time when the first-fruit of Romantic achievements had been harvested.

His approach throughout is axiomatic and without any argumentation. He does not waver in his decisions, and behind every quoted passage lurks his conviction that "it is the fact that . . . ". However, not infrequently, his personal comments are formulated very succinctly.

The emphasis of the essay is on imagination as Hunt sees it, and versification in the widest sense of the word, including rhyme, rhythm, and metre. Hunt illustrates his point amply with examples, and he goes into far greater detail – often down to the individual sounds of a line – than did either Wordsworth, Shelley or Coleridge.

What Is Poetry? cannot be called an original work, which becomes evident when, occasionally, Hunt ventures into theoretical reflections. Beauty, power, and truth are treated as the other Romanticists treated them: they are not defined – that would be a scientific approach entirely alien to Hunt and his contemporaries; their characteristics are shown indirectly, by means of exemplification. They are postulated as Absolutes, ideals to strive for, difficult to obtain, but more easily discernible once your attention has been made aware of them.

Thus, the criterion of truth is *accordance*: a statement is claimed to be true to the extent that it agreed with some unspecified abstract concept. The point is that Hunt and his contemporaries were at pains to maintain that the truth to be found in poetry was in no way inferior to that found in science. In poetry, truth was a matter of harmony between the poet's feeling and his expression.

Hunt's emphasis on the concept of power is equally symptomatic: power facilitates the poet's capacity of expression because he is in tune with one of the driving forces of the universe. The idea that the poet was a man specially privileged with not only a deep understanding of the secrets of the universe, but also with a talent of verbalizing those insights was prevalent in the beginning of the 19th century.

Hunt bolsters his presentation with great, seemingly incontrovertible abstracts with great extension but little precision. That goes for his use of the concept of pleasure, and the connotations of the idea of 'thought' vacillates between the negative and the positive. Also, when Hunt talks about variety as being equivalent to "pertinent diversity", it might be relevant to ask what "pertinent" actually means. Very often Hunt seems to be begging the question. Postulates abound, but on the other hand Hunt's repeated, but slightly changing use of some concepts, e.g. power, enables the reader to get an idea of what he is getting at. Nor should it be forgotten that Hunt is not the only Romanticist who is weak on precise terminology.

It will have appeared that the essay is not, nor does it pretend to be, a profoundly theoretical treatise. It is certainly not an *ars poetica.* Thus, no critic of poetry is quoted, no critical statement is analysed and no critical theory presented. Hunt has a *very* broad definition of the term imagination, which, in his idiolect, seems to be a psychological entity plus a particular talent and the result of a process. He offers a watered-out version of Coleridge's distinction He makes light of fancy, and he blurs the distinction between fancy and imagination. It is as if he writes within a paradigm that makes it compulsory for a discussion of poetry to observe, and comment on, that dichotomy, and he pays lip-service to it, but no more. He develops the two terms in a direction that was only hinted by Coleridge: Imagination is a quality that characterizes good poetry, whereas less good, or inferior, poetry falls under the heading of fancy.

Such didacticism as is found in the essay is implicit – there is no raised forefinger to the target group, who would probably not benefit very much from dry-as-dust sermonizing. Even worse, it might deprive "the general reader" of the "pleasure and exaltation" which Hunt saw it as the principal purpose of literature to convey.

Does he answer the question of the title? At least he tried to convey an idea of what *he* thought poetry was. For, obviously, the essay deals with "poetry as I see it". There is a curious discrepancy here between Hunt's talent of spotting quality in other authors and the not infrequent mediocrity of his own output. He wrote the essay because "poetry has been to me 'its own exceeding great reward'", as he says towards the end, quoting Bacon. The content of poetry to him was concerned with immediate sense experiences. He was not a nature mystic like Wordsworth – lakes and mountains did not appeal to him – and he was not a philosopher-cum-poet like Coleridge and, to some extent, Shelley. In most cases, his examples are expected to speak for themselves – to himself their impact was obvious, and he probably thought that too much construing would strip them of their poetical fragrance.

He goes straight to the point: dear reader, what I bring you here is poetry. It is obviously a case of showing rather than telling. Thus he gives a kind of indirect answer to the question posed by the title of the essay: he quotes numerous examples of what he considers good poetry and passes such theoretical reflections and deductions as may be required on to the reader. He does not spoon-feed the reader, and he certainly does not pontificate.

V

Hunt's Literary Credo

The essay *What is Poetry?* is one of Hunt's few attempts at sustained theorizing. It is an idiosyncratic work in the sense that the ideas it propounds and the attitude it expresses are clearly recognizable as Hunt's: we meet them again and again in his essays and translations and *obiter dicta* on his own poetry as well as that of other poets.

What Hunt is primarily concerned with is the finished product, and to him a poem is primarily an assembly of harmonious sounds, not an intellectual achievement. The idea of harmony was to a considerable extent typical of the age in which he wrote, but Hunt is alone in virtually excluding any other ingredient. Neither inspiration nor the creative process (like Wordsworth's "emotion recollected in tranquillity") interested him, and he never refers to any subject or situation as being specifically poetic (such as heroic deeds, national uplift, man's happiness or misery, a sunset near the sea, the beauty of a country girl, etc.). It seems that, according to him, anything under the sun might be a suitable poetical subject. It was the linguistic aspect of poetry that absorbed him, ranging from the individual line to the page-long passage of successful lines. The poetical effect is not so much achieved by the individual metaphor as by a concatenation of striking images. But then again, Hunt does not analyse the concept of metaphor – perhaps he thought that the more comprehensive term 'image', which he uses to cover all kinds of poetical ornament, would suffice for his target group. Hunt was convinced that man's inherent nature has a need of "ornament",[1] and to him literature primarily meant poetry. "I write with the greatest composure in verse," he says in his autobiography. He writes his poems slowly, "the musical form is a perpetual solace and refinement".[2] His main interest where poetry was concerned was versification, but he found interest in versification sadly lacking in his own age; he was sure that *The Story of Rimini* had been misjudged on that score.

Hunt's style is always, as in *What Is Poetry?*, digressive. In his numerous theatrical reviews and the essays of his periodicals he very often loses sight of his subject. Many of his prose writings begin promisingly, i.e. with a point he wishes to discuss, but his lateral thinking soon leads him astray.

To Hunt, versification was essentially a matter of rhythm – the alternation of weak and strong syllables and the ensuing harmonious synthesis. "A true lover of nature . . . is . . . pleased with harmonious variety", he says in his autobiography.[3] The idea that *concordia discors* is a given in the natural order of things is also fundamental to his life-long loving interest in music. He stated that an ear for music, and at least some professional insight into music, were a *sine qua non* for a poet.

Hunt's attitude to the role of thought in poetry and literature remained ambivalent throughout his life. In an article in the *Examiner* from December 1, 1816 (i.e. when he was a fairly young man) he calls attention to the recent emergence of what he calls a new school within poetry. Basically, that school restores "the same love of nature, and of *thinking* instead of mere *talking*, which formerly rendered us real poets and not merely versifying wits, and bead rollers of couplets"; the allusion to Pope and his school is obvious.

However, in his evaluation of Keats in his later work *Imagination and Fancy*, Hunt relegates thought to a place behind and beneath feeling: he praises Keats for not spending too much effort on thinking, "and thus should other young poets draw upon the prominent points of their feelings upon a subject, sucking the essence out of them into analogous words, instead of beating about the bush for *thoughts,* and, perhaps getting clever ones, but not thoroughly pertinent, not wanted, not the best. Such, at least, is the difference between the truest poetry and the degrees beneath it".[4] Like Rousseau, he found feeling the be-all and end-all of life, and he does not contribute to the discussion about the role of reason in the creation of poetry to which some of the other Romantic poets devoted some energy.

The passage about "analogous words" is one that a modern reader would have liked to see elaborated. A poem, like any work of art, is feeling given form. What Hunt suggests here is that a given feeling has a verbal equivalent. The thorny and crucial problem of how to verbalize feeling, how to account for the leap between abstract (feeling) and concrete (word), has been tackled very tentatively by poets and critics down through the ages, including Hunt's own contemporaries. Coleridge addressed the question in his preface to *Kubla* Khan: " . . . if that indeed can be called composition in which all the images rose up before him as, with a parallel production of the correspondent expressions, without any sensation or consciousness of effort."[5] The implication is that in that case there was a spontaneous harmony between feeling and word. Shelley was primarily concerned with the mission of poetry, not its verbalization. The soaring idealism of *A Defence of Poetry* never touched ground level. In a letter to Hitchener (7 January 1812) he writes: "Think of the poetry which I have inserted as a picture of my feelings, not a specimen of my art."[6] And even if Wordsworth devotes many lines to the language of poetry in his *Preface*, he did not go into any detail about the process that transforms emotions into words. His "spontaneous overflow" seemed in itself to guarantee that the appropriate words would come up.

In the poem *I Wandered Lonely As a Cloud* he "gazed – and gazed", at a host of golden daffodils, "but little thought/What wealth the show to me had brought". "For oft when on my couch I lie/In vacant or in pensive mood/They flash upon that inward eye/Which is the bliss of solitude". The sight "my heart with plea-sure fills", and, we are to understand, has furnished material for the poem. A sight "recollected in tranquillity" leads – inexplicably, spontaneously and unswervingly right – to the writing of a poem. No further explanation is given. The reason may be, as he says in the prefatory note to *Ode: Intimations of Immortality* that he did not conceive of "internal" and "external" as two rigidly separated compartments.

Poets in general seem to subscribe to Cato the Elder's first rule for orators: *"rem tene, et verba sequentur"* (get hold of the matter, and words will follow). Romantic theorists were aware of, and concerned with, the contrast between subconscious inspiration, which gave harmonious and perfect verses, and the artistic technique which endeavoured to give adequate expression to the original idea without spoiling it. Mostly they did not believe in the "natural" creation of masterpieces without the intervention of the intellect. But they hardly ever got down to an analysis of what bridged the gap, also because, as has been mentioned earlier, their terminology is not as clear as could be wished. They had no theoretical instruments to enable them to account for the correspondence between feeling and expression. (Nor had Cato!). All Romantic poets took it for granted that it was the poet's prerogative to find *le mot juste*: the poet was a person whose mental equipment made the transition from feeling to expression smooth and unproblematic.

In the above passage, Hunt dug one spit deeper and tried to bridge the gap by suggesting an analogy between feeling and word. His thought bears some resemblance to T. S. Eliot's theory of the "objective correlative", which he advanced in the essay *Hamlet and His Problems* (1919): in order to express an emotion in art, the artist must find an objective correlative, i.e. "a set of objects, a situation, a chain of events, which shall be the formula of that particular emotion", and which will then evoke the corresponding emotion in the reader. Even if Eliot does not refer specifically to words as objective correlatives, later critics have read that into his theory.

According to Eliot, a poem should not be a direct subjective expression of the poet's state of mind, but an organization that stands for the poet's emotion, a structure which is an external equivalent of an internal state of mind. Paradoxically, the target of Eliot's attack was poets who wallowed in their own emotions – and those poets included not only several of the Romantic poets, but also Hunt himself.

The theory has been hotly debated. It has been argued that any emotion can be rendered by a large number of words (e.g. love or horror), and that it is difficult to see how complex or mixed feelings can be incorporated in the theory. Of course any artist must create the combination that will produce the effect he desires. However, Eliot is not very explicit about the nature of the structure that is supposed to produce a given state of mind. Hunt wanted the reader to share the genuine pleasure he felt when reading poetry, and for that purpose he suggested – in what is little more than an off-hand remark – that some words were more suitable than others, which is not a very original idea. Regrettably, he leaves the discussion at that.

The "analogy" idea takes its place among his many *obiter dicta* which are potentially of absorbing interest, and which make some passages of *What Is Poetry?* intriguing reading, but which are allowed to remain rudimentary approaches.

Hunt never abandoned the idea of poetry as a linguistic pursuit. "Thus it is that poetry, in its intense sympathy with creation, may be said to create anew, rendering its words more impressive than the objects they speak of, and individually more lasting."[7] The words of poetry enables the reader to see familiar things in a new light – not a very sensational statement, but a favourite Romantic idea.

However, occasionally he also claimed that literature, and especially poetry, might have a social impact by influencing the legislative processes of society so as to improve man's situation, an optimistic idea that had been provoked by the frightening consequences of the incipient Industrial Revolution, and which is found in embryo in both Wordsworth's, Shelley's and Coleridge's theoretical speculations. What surprises a modern reader is that he tends to downplay the role of metaphor in the creative process, which means that he does not really come to grips with one of the central issues in Romantic thinking.

Conclusion

It was Wordsworth and Coleridge who were instrumental in directing poetical discussion towards a concentration on language, versification, and rhythm.

Wordsworth published his poetical theory in the form of a preface: his *Preface to the Second Edition of Lyrical Ballads* (1800) advanced an idiosyncratic and untenable theory about the language of poetry, where he made himself the spokesman of a change of paradigm after the "poetic diction" of much 18th century poetry. However, the experiences he chose as material for his poetry are not easy to put into words. It is true that he wrote about simple people, but the experience he derived from meeting them was one of aesthetic intuition.

He is the originator of the distinction between imagination and fancy. By imagination the Romanticists understood a power or talent that intuitively perceives an order, a law, a harmony, an awareness of the unity behind the chaotic "reality", a faculty that convinces the mind of the reality of the ideal, and which prompts some men to formulate this ideal in words.[1] However, as has already been suggested, the Romanticists' acknowledgement of, and dependence on, the intellectual powers of the mind should not be undervalued. Shelley's outburst against the intellect in *A Defence of Poetry* does not epitomize his attitude, cf. the *Hymn to Intellectual Beauty*: "I vowed that I would dedicate my powers/To thee and thine – have I not kept my vow?" For by imagination they did not understand a power that gave a free rein to any idea that happened to come into the poet's mind. Hunt's idiosyncratic use of the concept in *What Is Poetry?* goes far beyond the use his contemporaries made of it.

Wordsworth's distinction between imagination and fancy occurs in what is little more than an off-hand remark, and, like Hunt, he uses the two terms as criteria of poetic quality. If he can be said at all to address the question of what poetry is, he goes about it in an indirect way.

In *Biographia Literaria* (1817), Coleridge gives an account of his philosophical development and his present position. It is a very personal document, meant as an explanation rather than a defence. In the first part Coleridge describes his indebtedness to, and objections against, certain German philosophers and propounds his ground-breaking distinction between Imagination and Fancy, which has been influential in discussions of matters poetical ever since. Coleridge was aware that the law of association goes back to Aristotle, but he was violently opposed to Hartley's theory of association, and he used many pages to reject it. Actually, *Biographia Literaria* is a landmark in English poetry for its breach with association psychology. Coleridge's point was that merely mechanical association leads to a qualitatively inferior category of poetry because it is characterized by fancy. In 1810, he wrote to Crabb Robinson that fancy is "the arbitrary bringing together of things that lie remote and forming them into a unity". It "acts by a sort of juxtaposition".[2]

Hunt adopts the distinction – *What Is Poetry* appeared in a work entitled *Imagination and Fancy* – but perhaps it was convention rather than inclination that impelled him. The question is whether he actually understood Coleridge's argumentation or just employed a ready-made paradigm. At least he used the terms far more loosely than Coleridge had done. But Coleridge does not, in *Biographia Literaria*, pronounce on what poetry is. His focus lay elsewhere, and throughout he endeavours to clarify the meaning and the implications of the terms he uses.

Shelley wrote *A Defence of Poetry* in 1822 (it was not published until 1840, i.e. posthumously) because he felt it incumbent upon him to defend poets and poetry against attacks levelled against them, down through the centuries, for immorality. The book is also a reply to Peacock's *The Four* Ages from 1820, which held that poetry plays a less prominent role in an advanced society than in a primitive one. Like Hunt, Shelley believed in the socially restorative powers of literature. *A Defence of* Poetry, which is heavily indebted to Plato's idea of poetic inspiration, is an array of positively loaded superlatives about the divine nature of poetry, the benefits it confers on mankind, and the impeccable morality of poets. But Shelley also recognizes that art forms are the product of a given period and a culture. The reader looks in vain for any argumentation, and Shelley makes no attempt to win over doubters and sceptics.

His flowery terminology is as muddled as Hunt's, but, unlike Hunt, he is skimpy with exemplification. It is Shelley's contention that humanity cannot live without poetry, indeed that mankind has actually been more enriched by poetry than by philosophy or natural science. He underlines the significance of imagination ("Poetry, in a general sense, may be defined to be 'the expression of the imagination'"), and he stresses the unconscious element in art: "Poetry . . . differs in this respect from logic that it is not subject to the control of the active powers of the mind, and that its birth and recurrence have no necessary connexion with the consciousness or will."[3] Yet, towards the end of the essay, he, like Hunt, acknowledges the merits of science.

Unlike his three contemporaries, Hunt faces the issue squarely in the very title of his essay. In its construction, *What Is Poetry?* shares some features with famous *artes poeticae* like Aristotle's *Poetics* and Horace's *Ars poetica*: But whereas Aristotle had *defined* what a tragedy is, Hunt's emphasis is on a collection of *examples* of what, in his opinion, good poetry is. The essay *What Is Poetry* appeared in a book the full title of which is *Imagination and Fancy, or Selections from the English Poets, Illustrative of those First Requisites of their Art; with Markings of the Best Passages, Critical Notes of the Writers, and an Essay in Answer to the Question What Is Poetry*. Like his two famous predecessors, Hunt also gives a characterization of the good poet and an account of the purpose of poetry.

But *What Is Poetry?* is not – and is not intended to be – an *ars poetica* in the conventional sense. On the other hand, it is more than a commented anthology of purple patches. It is a child of its age and differs in virtually every respect from for example, the Neo-classicists' didactic reflections on poetry and literature. Hunt did not enjoin poets to follow certain rules derived from Antiquity and Renaissance theorists – he expressly praises Spenser for breaking any rules – nor did he advise poets to imitate models like Homer and Horace. Taste and judgement are given short shrift, and conceits may even in "subtle thinkers show lack of taste" (Hunt instances Donne). Unlike the Neo-Classicists, Hunt and the other Romantic poets were not interested in compartmentalization and hierarchization, and such rules or axioms as they referred to were extrapolations of their own experiences and idiosyncracies. Like his Romantic contemporaries, Hunt saw the poet as a uniquely gifted human being, and he looked upon the material world as a concrete manifestation, but alas! also a faint reflection, of a higher "spiritual" reality lying behind.

In 1803, Coleridge had written an essay, *Concerning Poetry and the Pleasure to be Derived from it*, but that work has not got nearly the same degree of spontaneous enthusiasm as Hunt's essay.

What Is Poetry? distinguishes itself from that work as well as from the three other theoretical works described above. Hunt was not a nature mystic like Wordsworth, and he was decidedly uncomfortable with the subjects that the authors he called "the Lake Poets" chose for their poetry. He was ambivalent with regard to the role of thought in poetry, and his beauty was a far cry from Shelley's intellectual variant. Coleridge's German-inspired transcendental philosophy was far beyond Hunt – and the readers for whom his essay was intended. Hunt was not interested in the act of creation as Wordsworth was ("emotion recollected in tranquility"). Actually he was more in line with the latter's characterization of poetry as "the spontaneous overflow of powerful feelings" and especially with Wordsworth's statement in the Preface to the effect that the end of poetry is pleasure –

"the grand elementary principle of pleasure," as Wordsworth puts it.

To Hunt, poetry is not marked by the characteristics of the age in which it was written. Poetry is poetry for all seasons – euphony, not didacticism, loyalty to the poet's feelings rather than "truth to nature" or imitation of models from Classical Antiquity. Nor is poetry dependent on its subject in the sense that some subjects lend themselves more willingly to poetic treatment than others. Beauty is not moral uplift, but mellifluous versification and a rhythm characterized by *concordia discors*.

But that is not all: there is far less sustained argumentation in Hunt than in Coleridge. His treatment of the role of thought in poetry is a symptomatic example in that it shows him as a muddled thinker. Hunt often starts off as if he intends to pursue an idea, but he soon drops it, or is content with giving confusing illustrations of it. On the other hand, he goes far more into detail with regard to vocabulary, metre, rhythm, and versification than they do. Actually, in many passages Hunt practises what we would call today close reading. He participated whole-heartedly in the Romanticists' reaction against what they called the monotony ("see-saw") of the verse written by the school of Pope. All that he wrote shows unmistakably that monotony was anathema to him. His theory of alternating rhythm – variety in uniformity – is ultimately rooted in his conception of pleasure as the aim of poetry and, more generally, literature – and life, it might be added. And he projected his own boredom with rigid regularity and uniformity on to the reader, to whom he attributed his own likes and dislikes.

Hunt's great achievement in *What Is Poetry?* is that he attempts to address the issue from the reader's point of view. None of the other theorists had done that with the possible exception of what Coleridge did in his prose comments in the margin of *The Ancient Mariner*. Hunt never loses sight of his reader – he wrote *for* "the common man", whereas Wordsworth wrote *about* simple people. That is the reason for Hunt's generous supply of examples from different centuries: he adopts a pedagogical, almost taking-by-the-hand, approach, whereas the other theorists wrote for a well-read audience – or for each other. Hunt had no personal axe to grind, and it can be plausibly suggested that the construction and set-up of the text is an illustration of the tendency towards democratization that was part and parcel of the Romantic *Zeitgeist*.

Hunt's essay is not the ultimate Romantic treatment of the subject of poetry. His evaluations are based on his own intuitions plus the broad basis he had acquired in his extensive reading of English and foreign literature. And it was that basis that made his intuition more than random caprices.

It is not only *What Is Poetry?* that had the general reader as its target group In his theatrical reviews, too, Hunt wrote for the interested layman. His articles are often hastily written, but frequently with one or two interesting comments on the way (e.g. on the masque and on the pantomime),[4] and he concentrated on single features of the performance rather than on the plays as a whole. As was the case with poetry, he knew quality when he saw it, but he considered the art of acting as something to be admired and described, but not analysed. He was aware that many of his verdicts were idiosyncratic dixits, but he defended his position by referring to Dr Johnson, who was "careless of all proof".[5]

Hunt was an indefatigable, though not overly successful, editor of periodicals, which were nearly all of them short-lived. Their titles are indicative of their content: the *Examiner,* the *Tatler,* the *Liberal,* the *Reflector* (which means both 'mirror' and 'thinker'), the *Indicator* ("after a bird of that name who shows people where to find wild honey," Hunt writes in a letter to Shelley on 20th September 1819).[6] The OED calls the bird the "honey-guide".

As a matter of fact, they might all be given the title that Hunt gave to a periodical which he started in 1834, and which had to cease publication in the following year, viz. *Leigh Hunt's London Journal.* In each of the periodicals Hunt seemed convinced that his contemporaries felt a strong need to hear what *he* had to say. He was the main, sometimes the sole, contributor to those publications, and he always considered the needs and the scope of his target group. Hunt appears mostly as the benevolent, chatty and patient, but not unduly patronizing educator. Drama is, as he sees it, "the first of moralities" because it gives us knowledge of ourselves. But he also admits that little in the contemporary theatre lives up to any high moral standards. However, theatre is not his main point; his articles mostly deal with current affairs, discuss the talk of the town, print excerpts from, and call their readers' attention to, classical literature as well as more recent publications. There are sometimes lengthy accounts of the plots of current plays, told with many digressions and winks at the reader, but he avoids the abstract aesthetic concerns of Coleridge. His love and understanding of books and literature is evident everywhere in his periodicals. But there are also instances of satirical or vituperative attacks on what he considered political ineptitude, or even oppression. Thus, on numerous occasions he gives vent to his profound indignation at the licentiousness of the Prince Regent – a feeling that was shared by most of his contemporaries.

The prefaces of the periodicals, which are so many declarations of content, are tailored to one and the same pattern. As we saw in *What Is Poetry?*, the purpose of poetry was held to convey pleasure, and actually 'pleasure' and 'entertainment' and their synonyms are the most frequently occurring words in the prefaces of Hunt's periodicals.

The *Examiner*, whose first number appeared in 1804, differs from the rest in being more politically outspoken than the other periodicals. Its articles were very much influenced by the utilitarianism of Jeremy Bentham, who was a highly respected polemicist, and who visited Hunt both before his trial in 1812 and during his imprisonment. There is little doubt that Bentham's insistence on a reform of the legal system (*Introduction to the Principles of Morals and Legislation*, 1817) had a profound influence on Hunt. Bentham's conviction that he had "powers deeply to interest, or substantially to improve, mankind", as he wrote to Hunt in 1816,[7] appealed to Hunt's reformist zeal. The *Examiner* preached freedom in poetry as well as politics at the same time as it intended to locate "the beautiful" in life and art.

It is a recurrent feature for the articles in Hunt's periodicals to deplore the current low level of art, especially poetry. But they also contain material that would today be subsumed under the heading of small talk. Thus, the *Indicator* will "deal with any subject falling within the scope of the editor's knowledge"; it promises to show its readers what is worth occupying themselves with. The purpose of the *Reflector* is – as suggested by the title – to consider its own and other people's opinions. The *Tatler* aims at giving entertaining excerpts from books in order to initiate its readers into "pleasant and improving thoughts".

Apart from the *Examiner*, all the periodicals had to be discontinued after a short time, sometimes little more than a year. Even if contributions by Lamb and Hazlitt raised the standard and roused the readers' interest, the financial sources quickly dried up. Yet the current attempts at rehabilitating Hunt see him as a perspicacious observer and a very influential participant in the political debate of his age. That would seem to be stating the case a little too strongly.

It has been argued that Hunt is just a man who has the good fortune to find himself at the top of the wave of Romantic poetry without himself being a first-rate poet, and that he is no more than an uninteresting person living in interesting times, among interesting people. Obviously, such statements only contain part of the truth. Rather, it seems, his poetical oeuvre is evidence of the incipient decline of the Romantic movement. Blunden says that "men of dawning ability seem to have come into his life at different times".[8] Even his contemporary friends occasionally hinted that he was fortunate enough to be at the right place at the right moment, and even his most benevolent well-wishers admitted that he himself was partly to blame for the hardships he encountered. As he grew older, he became a curious mixture of a grey eminence and a quaint anachronism – most of the really great Romantic poets had died, but Hunt had outlived them and could reminisce about them, which was an attraction to some of his contemporaries. The ideals he and others had fought for were on the wane. But Hunt stuck to them and was rewarded, in some circles, with slightly baffled or embarrassed respect.

By literature Hunt understood poetry. James Mill (John Stuart Mill's father) had also argued that "the first literature is poetry. Poetry is the language of the passions, and men feel before they speculate".[9] To Hunt, essays were runners-up, but the irony is that, by and large, he was better at writing essays than poems. In his youth he wrote a good many novels, but they hardly ever figure in the list of his publications. Characteristically, the half-baked literary hierarchy he establishes at some point in *What is Poetry?* deals exclusively with "kinds" (as the Neo-Classicists called them) of poetry. On one occasion, however, he shows a clear perception of how a novelist should treat reality. Using Lytton's *Eugène Aram* as his example, Hunt says that a novelist is allowed to add material, but not to change reality.[10] A similar thought occurs in his discussion of imagination in *What Is Poetry?*: a poet should beware of going too far beyond reality and never create beings or situations that reality would not approve of.

Intellectual conversation, some works of art and, to some extent, aspects of nature started something in him, and he described his reactions with rapt enthusiasm – and, it must be added, sometimes with moderate information value. His criticism was achronical: he assumed that people's ideals of beauty remain unchanged down through the centuries, just as he held that good poetry is good, irrespective of the age in which it was written. Accordingly he had no qualms with viewing poets of earlier ages through the eyes of his own day. He ignores Spenser's world picture and Dante's theology, and he made no secret of the fact that he was incapable of understanding Sir Thomas Browne's thinking. Yet he admired their works. Orwell said about Dickens that he is better in his parts than in his wholes. That characterization is eminently applicable to Hunt.

For he is not without critical acumen: his criticism of

Wordsworth's *Peter Bell* is incisive. Also, he held that it was an asset for an author to write both "gay and grave", which Shakespeare could do, but Milton could not.[11] There are even occasional – admittedly very occasional – glimpses of humour in his evaluations, as when he says that Tennyson's women most of all resemble poetical seamstresses.

Whereas he did reach some sort of theological serenity when he grew older, his reflections on, and life-long occupation with, literature never led this "last survivor of a race of giants" to take an ultimate and reasonably well-defined stand. He was not a theory-builder, but nor were Keats and Shelley. His achievement – apart from his gift as a talent scout and his altruistic assistance to budding geniuses – was that he strove to put his enormous, if erratic, learning at the disposal of ordinary people. He did not write for a coterie of fellow poets, literary critics or intellectual highbrows. In the Preface to the *Examiner* he defines style with his characteristic vagueness as "proper words in proper places", and in all that he wrote his aim was to make his "proper words" palatable to the uninitiated. He knew himself that he did not always succeed.

The perspicacious Amy Lowell, who has an almost uncanny talent of succinct characterization, called him "not a great creator, but a great introducer". That hits the nail on the head.

Notes

Preface

1 Anthony Holden, *The Wit in the Dungeon* (Little Brown, 2005), p. x.
2 Ibid., p. 2.
3 Ibid., p. ix.

Chapter I The Man

1 *The Autobiography of Leigh Hunt; with Reminiscences of Friends and Contemporaries* (London, 1850).
2 Ibid., p. 1.
3 Ibid., pp. 149–51.
4 Ibid., p. 371.
5 Ibid., p. 401.
6 Ibid., p. 402.
7 Ibid.
8 Ibid., p. 409.
9 Brimley Johnson, *Shelley–Leigh Hunt: How Friendship Made History* (London: Ingpen & Grant, 1928), p. 93.
10 Ibid., p. 117.

Chapter II Hunt's Relationship with Some of the Romantic Poets

1 Brimley Johnson, *Shelley–Leigh Hunt: How Friendship Made History* (London: Ingpen & Grant, 1928), p. 93.
2 Ibid., p. 117.
3 Nicholas Roe (ed.), *Leigh Hunt: Life, Poetics, Politics* (London: Routledge, 2003), p. 183
4 Johnson, *Shelley–Leigh Hunt*, p. 136.
5 Ibid., p. 141.
6 Ann Blainey, *Immortal Boy: A Portrait of Leigh Hunt* (London and Sydney: Croom Helm, 1985), p. 149.

7   *The Autobiography of Leigh Hunt; with Reminiscences of Friends and Contemporaries* (London, 1850), p. 149.

8   Leigh Hunt, *Imagination and Fancy; or Selections from the English Poets* 3rd ed. (London, 1846), p. 231.

9   Barnettie Miller, *Leigh Hunt's Relations with Byron, Shelley and Keats* (New York: Columbia University Press, 1910), p. 49.

10 Edmund Blunden, *Leigh Hunt: A Biography* (London: Cobden-Sanderson, 1930), p. 115.

11 Miller, *Leigh Hunt's Relations with Byron, Shelley and Keats*, p. 147.

12 Ibid., p. 254.

13 *The Autobiography of Leigh Hunt*, p. 254.

14 Hunt, *Imagination and Fancy*, p. 202.

15 R. Brimley Johnson (ed.), *Prefaces by Leigh Hunt: Mainly to his Periodicals* (Port Washington, New York: Kennical Press Inc., 1927, reissued 1967), p. 21.

16 *The Autobiography of Leigh Hunt*, p. 200.

17 Louis Landré, Louis, *Leigh Hunt (1784–1859). Contribution à l'histoire du romantisme anglais. Vol. I : L'auteur; vol. II : L'oeuvre* (Paris: Société d'Edition «Les Belles Lettres», 1935–36), vol. I, p. 193.

18 Philip Connell, *Romanticism, Economics, and the Question of 'Culture'* (Oxford University Press, 2001), p. 225.

19 Ibid., p. 232.

20 Marilyn Butler, *Romantics, Rebels and Reactionaries* (Oxford University Press, 1981), pp. 116–17.

21 Ibid., p. 120.

Chapter III Hunt's *What is Poetry?*

1   *What is Poetry?* in Leigh Hunt, *Imagination and Fancy; or Selections from the English Poets* 3rd ed. (London, 1846), p. 47.

2   Ibid., p. 2.

3   Ibid., p. ix.

4   Ibid., p. 2.

5   Ibid., p. 1.

6   S. T. Coleridge, *Biographia Literaria* (ed. J. Shawcross) (Oxford University Press, 1967).

7   Hunt, *What is Poetry?*, p. 2.

8   Ibid. p. 46.

9   Ibid.

10 Ibid., p. 47.

11 Ibid., p. 2.

12 Ibid., p. 4.

13 Ibid., p. 3.

14 Ibid., p. 45.

15 Ibid., p. 4.

16 Ibid., p. 3.

17 Ibid.

18 Ibid.

19 Ibid.

20 Ibid., p. 46.

21 William Wordsworth, *Preface to the Second Edition of Several of the Foregoing Poems Published with an Additional Volume under the Title of Lyrical Ballads (1802)*. The Norton Anthology of English Literature, vol. 2 (New York: W.W. Norton & Company Inc., 1968), p. 108.

22 Percy Bysshe Shelley, *A Defence of Poetry*. The Norton Anthology of English Literature, vol. 2 (New York: W.W. Norton & Company, 1968), p. 495.

23 *What Is Poetry?*, p. 2.

24 Ibid.

25 Wordsworth, *Preface to the Second Edition . . .* , p. 107.

26 Ibid., p. ix.

27 Coleridge, *Biographia Literaria I*, p. 202.

28 Ibid.

29 *What Is Poetry?*, p. 22.

30 Ibid.

31 Ibid., p. 34.

32 Ibid., p. 2.

33 Ibid., pp. 21–22.

34 Ibid., p. 2.

35 Ibid., pp. 5–6.

36 Ibid., p. 47.

37 Ibid., p. 2.

38 Ibid., p. 8.

39 Ibid.

40 Ibid., p. 13.

41 Ibid.
42 Ibid.
43 Ibid., p. 12.
44 Ibid., p. 20.
45 Ibid.
46 Ibid., p. 29.
47 Ibid., p. 20.
48 *Preface to the Second Edition . . .* , p. 103.
49 *What Is Poetry?*, p. 19.
50 *Preface to the Second Edition . . .* , p. 103.
51 *What Is Poetry?*, p. 44.
52 Ibid., p. 34.
53 Ibid.
54 Ibid., p. 44.
55 Ibid., p. 34.
56 Ibid., p. 2.
57 Ibid., p. 20.
58 Ibid.
59 Ibid., p. 22.
60 Ibid.
61 Ibid.
62 Ibid., p. 23.
63 Ibid., p. 21.
64 *Biographia Literaria I*, p. 202.
65 Ibid., p. 1.
66 Roe, *Leigh Hunt: Life, Poetics, Politics*, p. 244.
67 Blunden, *Leigh Hunt*, p. 101.
68 *What Is Poetry?*, p. 8.
69 Ibid., p. 2.
70 Ibid., pp. 4–5.
71 Ibid., p. 25.
72 Ibid.
73 Ibid., p. 26.
74 Ibid., p. 25.
75 Ibid., p. 41.
76 Ibid., p. 25.
77 Ibid.

78 Ibid.
79 Ibid., p. 26.
80 Ibid.
81 Ibid., p. 28.
82 Ibid., p. 30.
83 Ibid., p. 33.
84 Ibid.
85 Ibid., p. 30.
86 Horace, *Epistles*, I, xii, 19.
87 *What Is Poetry?*, p. 29.
88 Ibid., p. 24.
89 Ibid., p. 26.
90 Ibid., p. 27.
91 Ibid., p. 34.
92 Ibid.
93 Ibid., p. 35.
94 Ibid.
95 Ibid., p. 39.
96 Ibid., p. 41.
97 Ibid.
98 Ibid., p. 43.
99 T. A. Moxon (ed.), *Aristotle's Poetics: Demetrius on Style* (Everyman's Library, Dent, 1943), XI, pp. 24–25.
100 *Ars poetica*, 333.
101 *What Is Poetry?*, p. 2.
102 *Preface to the Second Edition . . .* , p. 105.
103 Ibid.
104 *What Is Poetry?*, p. 47
105 Cf. Flemming Olsen, *Between Positivism and T. S. Eliot: Imagism and T. E. Hulme* (University Press of Southern Denmark, 2008).
106 *What Is Poetry?,* p. 1.
107 *Preface to the Second Edition . . .* , p. 107.
108 *What Is Poetry?*, p. 1.
109 Ibid., p. 25.
110 Ibid., p. 44.
111 Ibid., p. 48.
112 Ibid.
113 Ibid., p. 43.

114 Ibid.

Chapter V Hunt's Literary Credo

1 Lawrence Huston Houtchens & Carolyn Washburn Houtchens (eds), *Leigh Hunt's Literary Criticism* (New York: Columbia University Press, 1956), p. 241.
2 *The Autobiography of Leigh Hunt; with Reminiscences of Friends and Contemporaries* (London, 1850), p. 374.
3 Ibid.
4 Leigh Hunt, *Imagination and Fancy; or Selections from the English Poets* 3rd ed. (London, 1846), p. 244.
5 Albert Gérard, *L'idée romantique de la poésie en Angleterre: Etudes sur la théorie de la poésie chez Coleridge, Wordsworth, Keats et Shelley* (Paris: Société d'Edition «Les Belles Lettres», 1955), p. 270.
6 Ibid., p. 267.
7 Hunt, *Imagination and Fancy*, p. 248.

Conclusion

1 Albert Gérard, *L'idée romantique de la poésie en Angleterre: Etudes sur la théorie de la poésie chez Coleridge, Wordsworth, Keats et Shelley* (Paris: Société d'Edition «Les Belles Lettres», 1955), p. 349.
2 S. T. Coleridge, *Biographia Literaria* (ed. J. Shawcross) (Oxford University Press, 1967), *Preface, I*, p. 50.
3 Marilyn Butler, *Romantics, Rebels and Reactionaries* (Oxford University Press, 1981), p. 168.
4 Lawrence Huston Houtchens & Carolyn Washburn Houtchens (eds), *Leigh Hunt's Literary Criticism* (New York: Columbia University Press, 1956), pp. 116–32.
5 Ibid., p. 38.
6 Brimley Johnson, *Shelley—Leigh Hunt: How Friendship Made History* (London: Ingpen & Grant, 1928), p. 123.
7 Philip Connell, *Romanticism, Economics, and the Question of 'Culture'* (Oxford University Press, 2001), p. 216.
8 Edmund Blunden, *Leigh Hunt. A Biography* (London: Cobden-Sanderson, 1930), p. 229.
9 Connell, *Romanticism, Economics, and the Question of 'Culture'*, p. 225.
10 Houtchens & Houtchens, *Literary Criticism*, pp. 349 et seq.
11 Ibid., pp. 559 et seq.

Bibliography

Blainey, Ann, *The Farthing Poet*. London, 1968.

———, *Immortal Boy. A Portrait of Leigh Hunt*. London and Sydney: Croom Helm, 1985.

Blunden, Edmund, *Leigh Hunt's "Examiner" Examined*. New York and London, 1928.

———, *Leigh Hunt and His Circle*. New York and London, 1930.

———, *Leigh Hunt: A Biography*. London: Cobden-Sanderson, 1930.

Brewer, L. A., *My Leigh Hunt Library: The Holograph Letters*. London, 1938.

Butler, Marilyn, *Romantics, Rebels and Reactionaries*. Oxford University Press, 1981.

Chambers, F. P., *The History of Taste*. Columbia University Press, 1932.

Clark, A. F. B., *Boileau and the French Classical Critics in England (1660–1830)*. Librairie Ancienne Edouard Champion, Paris, 1925.

Coleridge, S. T., *Biographia Literaria* (ed. J. Shawcross). Oxford University Press, 1967.

Connell, Philip, *Romanticism, Economics, and the Question of 'Culture'*. Oxford University Press, 2001.

Cox, Jeffrey, *Poetry and Politics in the Cockney School*. Cambridge University Press, 1998.

Eberle-Sinafra, Michael, *Leigh Hunt and the Literary Scene*. London: Routledge 2005.

Fenner, Theodore, *Leigh Hunt and Opera Criticism: The "Examiner" Years 1808-21*. University Press of Kansas, 1972.

Frye, Northrop (ed.), *Romanticism Reconsidered*. New York, 1963.

Gérard, Albert, *L'idée romantique de la poésie en Angleterre. Etudes sur la théorie de la poésie chez Coleridge, Wordsworth, Keats et Shelley*. Paris: Société d'Edition Les Belles Lettres, 1955.

Gilbert K. E. & Kuhn, H. A., *A History of Esthetics*. Indiana University Press, 1953.

Graham, Walter, *English Literary Periodicals*. New York, 1930.

Green, David Bonnell & Wilson, Edwin Graves (eds), *Keats, Shelley, Byron, Hunt and Their Circles*. Lincoln: University of Nebraska Press, 1964.

Hall, S. C., *Book of Gems*. London, 1838.

Holden, Anthony, *The Wit in the Dungeon: A Life of Leigh Hunt*. New York: Little, Brown, 2005.

Houtchens, Lawrence Huston & Houtchens, Caroline Washburn (eds), *Leigh Hunt's Dramatic Criticism*. New York: Columbia University Press, 1949.

Houtchens, Lawrence Huston & Houtchens, Carolyn Washburn (eds), *Leigh Hunt's Literary Criticism*. New York: Columbia University Press, 1956.

—— (eds), *Political Essays of Leigh Hunt*. New York: Columbia University Press, 1962

Hunt, Leigh, *Juvenalia, or a Collection of Poems*. London, 1802.

——, *Critical Essays on the Performers of the London Theatres*. London, 1807.

——, *The Examiner. A Sunday Paper on Politics, Domestic Economy, and Theatricals*. London, 1808 et seq.

——, *The Descent of Liberty. A Mask*. London, 1815.

——, *The Story of Rimini, a Poem*. London, 1816.

——, *Foliage, or Poems Original and Translated*. London, 1818.

——, *The Poetical Works of Leigh Hunt*. 3 vols. London, 1819.

——, *Amyntas, a Tale of the Woods; from the Italian of Torquato Tasso*. London 1820.

——, *Lord Byron and Some of his Contemporaries, with Recollections of the Author's Life and of his Visit to Italy*. Vols. 1–3. Paris, 1828.

——, *Sir Ralph Esher; or Memories of a Gentleman of the Court of Charles II*, 3 vols. London, 1830.

——, *Christianism; or Belief and Unbelief Reconciled*. London, 1832.

——, *The Indicator, and the Companion; a Miscellany for the Fields and the Fireside*, 2 vols. 1834.

——, *Captain Sword and Captain Pen. A Poem*. London, 1835.

——, *A Legend of Florence. A Play in Five Acts*. London, 1840.

——, *The Palfrey; a Love Story of Old Times*. London, 1842.

——, *Imagination and Fancy; or Selections from the English Poets*, 3rd ed. London, 1846.

——, *Wit and Humour. Selected from the English Poets, with an Illustrative Essay and Critical Comments.* London, 1846.

——, *Men, Women, and Books; a Selection of Sketches, Essays, and Critical Memoirs from his Uncollected Prose Writings.* London, 1847.

——, *The Town. Its Memorable Characters and Events. St Paul's to St. James's.* London, 1848.

——, *The Autobiography of Leigh Hunt; with Reminiscences of Friends and Contemporaries.* London, 1850.

——, *The Religion of the Heart. A Manual of Faith and Duty.* London, 1853.

——, *Stories in Verse. Now first Collected.* London, 1855.

——, *The Correspondence of Leigh Hunt. Edited by his Eldest Son,* 2 vols. London, 1860.

Hunt, T. (ed.), *The Poetical Works of Leigh Hunt.* London 1860.

Johnson, Edgar, *Charles Dickens: His Tragedy and Triumph.* London, 1953.

Johnson, R. Brimley (ed.), *Prefaces by Leigh Hunt. Mainly to his Periodicals.* New York, Port Washington: Kennical Press Inc., 1927, reissued 1967.

——, *Shelley–Leigh Hunt: How Friendship Made History.* London: Ingpen & Grant, London, 1928.

Jones, F. L. (ed.), *The Letters of Percy Bysshe Shelley,* 2 vols. Oxford: Clarendon, 1964.

Kendall, Kenneth E., *Leith Hunt's «Reflector».* University of Florida Press, 1971.

Kroeber, Karl, *Romantic Narrative Art.* Madison: University of Wisconsin Press, 1960.

Landré, Louis, *Leigh Hunt (1784–1859). Contribution à l'histoire du romantisme anglais. Vol. I : L'auteur; vol. II: L'oeuvre.* Société d'Edition «Les Belles Lettres», Paris, 1935–36.

Lucas, F. L., *The Decline and Fall of the Romantic Ideal.* Cambridge University Press, 1936.

Mahoney, Charles, *Romantics and Renegades: The Poetics of Political Reaction.* London: Palgrave Macmillan, 2002.

Marshall, William H., *Byron, Shelley, Hunt and The Liberal.* Philadelphia, 1960.

Merriam, Harold G., *Edward Moxon, Publisher of Poets.* New York: Columbia University Press, 1939.

Miller, Barnettie, *Leigh Hunt's Relations with Byron, Shelley and Keats.* New York: Columbia University Press, 1910.

Moxon, T. A. (ed.), *Aristotle's Poetics: Demetrius on Style* (Everyman's Library, Dent, 1943), XI, pp. 24–25.

Olsen, Flemming, *Between Positivism and T. S. Eliot: Imagism and T. E. Hulme.* University Press of Southern Denmark, 2008.

Robertson, J. G., *Studies in the Genesis of Romantic Theory in the Eighteenth Century.* Cambridge, 1923.

Roe, Nicholas (ed.), *Leigh Hunt: Life, Poetics, Politics.* London: Routledge, 2003.

——, *Fiery Heart: The First Life of Leigh Hunt.* Pimlico, 2005.

Saintsbury, George, *A Historical Manual of English Prosody.* London: Macmillan, 1923.

Sanders, Charles Richard, *The Correspondence and Friendship of Thomas Carlyle and Leigh Hunt.* The Jordan Rylands Library, Manchester, MCMLXIII.

Shannon, Edgar F., *Tennyson and the Reviewers.* Harvard University Press, 1952.

Shelley, Percy Bysshe, *A Defence of Poetry.* The Norton Anthology of English Literature, vol. 2. W.W. Norton & Company, New York, 1968.

Stout, George D., *The Political History of Leigh Hunt's "Examiner".* St. Louis: Washington University Studies, 1949.

Symons, Arthur (ed.), *The Essays of Leigh Hunt.* New York: Dutton 1890.

Tatchell, Molly, *Leigh Hunt and his Family in Hammersmith.* London 1969.

Watson, Melvin R., *Magazine Serials and the Essay Tradition 1746–1820.* Baton Rouge Louisiana State University Press, 1956.

Wordsworth, William, *Preface to the Second Edition of Several of the Foregoing Poems Published with an Additional Volume under the Title of Lyrical Ballads (1802).* The Norton Anthology of English Literature, vol. 2. W.W. Norton & Company Inc., 1968.

Index